Cantors

a collection of Gregorian chants

selected and edited by
MARY BERRY
Newnham College, Cambridge

with new English words for singing by
ROSE MARY McCABE

CAMBRIDGE UNIVERSITY PRESS
Cambridge
London · New York · Melbourne

The Resources of Music Series

General Editors: *Wilfrid Mellers, John Paynter*

THE RESOURCES OF MUSIC *by Wilfrid Mellers*
SOUND AND SILENCE *by John Paynter and Peter Aston* (recording available)
SOMETHING TO PLAY *by Geoffrey Brace*
MUSIC DRAMA IN SCHOOLS *edited by Malcolm John*
THE PAINFUL PLOUGH *by Roy Palmer*
THE VALIANT SAILOR *by Roy Palmer*
TROUBADOURS *by Brian Sargent* (recording available)
MINSTRELS *by Brian Sargent* (recording available)
POVERTY KNOCK *by Roy Palmer*
THE RIGS OF THE FAIR *by Roy Palmer and Jon Raven*
JAZZ *by Graham Collier* (recordings available)
POP MUSIC IN SCHOOL *edited by Graham Vulliamy and Ed Lee*
FOLK MUSIC IN SCHOOL *edited by Robert Leach and Roy Palmer*
VIBRATIONS *by David Sawyer*
MINSTRELS 2 *by Brian Sargent*
STRIKE THE BELL *by Roy Palmer*

Acknowledgements

Full source references to chants and sources of illustrations are listed on page 48. The author and publisher would like to thank all those there listed for permission to reproduce material in this book.

While every effort has been made to contact copyright holders, the publishers apologize if any material has been included without permission.

Performing and recording rights are reserved and are administered by the Performing Rights Society, The Mechanical Copyright Protection Society and the affiliated bodies throughout the world. Applications should be made to these bodies for a relevant licence. Failure to so apply constitutes a breach of copyright.

Front cover: Cantors singing at a feast-day service
Title page: Friars in choir

Published by the Syndics of the CAMBRIDGE UNIVERSITY PRESS
The Pitt Building, Trumpington Street, Cambridge CB2 1RP
Bentley House, 200 Euston Road, London NW1 2DB
32 East 57th Street, New York, NY 10022, USA
296 Beaconsfield Parade, Middle Park, Melbourne 3206, Australia

© Cambridge University Press 1979

First published 1979

Printed in Great Britain at the Alden Press, Oxford

Library of Congress Cataloguing in Publication Data
Main entry under title:
Cantors
(The Resources of music series)
Words in Latin and English.
Bibliography and discography: p.
Includes Index.
1. Chants (Plain, Gregorian, etc.) I. Berry,
Mary, 1917–
II. Catholic Church. Liturgy and ritual.
III. Series.
M2150.2.B47 1979   783.5'52   78-56178
ISBN 0 521 22149 8

Contents

Introduction	4
Music round the year	
1 An Advent hymn *Conditor alme siderum*	11
2 A Christmas antiphon *Hodie Christus*	12
3 A processional chant for Candlemas *Lumen*	13
4 A hymn for the cross *Vexilla regis*	15
5 An Easter responsory *Surrexit Dominus*	16
6 Two Easter versicles	17
7 A hymn to the Holy Spirit *Veni creator*	18
The languages of the chant	
8 Kyrie *Orbis factor*	19
9 The Trisagion from the Good Friday Liturgy	20
10 Three Easter Alleluias	21
Hours of the day and moments of life	
11 A morning hymn *Jam lucis*	23
12 An evening hymn *Te lucis*	24
13 A Gregorian grace before meals	25
14 Two prayers of thanksgiving	26
15 A Christmas hymn *Puer natus*	27
16 Two antiphons for the dead — for the funeral of Phyllyp Sparowe	28
17 A funeral chant *In paradisum*	29
The song school	
18 A scripture reading	30
19 A medieval teaching aid *Ut queant laxis*	32
20 A psalm *Laudate Dominum*	34
21 *Alma Redemptoris Mater*	35
Instruments	
22 A motto for an organ loft	37
23 An instrumental plainsong *In Nomine*	38
Pageantry	
24 The Laudes regiae, or Royal Acclamations *Christus vincit*	41
Suggestions for further activities	
Background reading	46
Records	47
Sources	48

Introduction

A medieval cantor would have known by heart all the music of the services that used to be sung in the parish church, or cathedral, or monastery, or royal chapel in which he served. It would have been his job to sing at all the services which went on round the clock, day and night, in medieval times. There might have been as many as eight of them in one day, and they were especially brilliant and solemn on great festivals such as Christmas or Easter. He would have sung the very simple chants he had been taught in the song school, and also the more elaborate ones, taking the solo parts and leading the other members of the choir in singing the psalms and the hymns. The music would have been familiar to everybody: it was quite as well known as the theme music of a popular TV series is to-day. Everyone would have recognized the different chants, which would have reminded them of the occasion that was being celebrated. For not only was there special music for the different feasts of the year, but also for the different hours of the day; there was music for rejoicing and music for mourning; music for greeting the king or the bishop, and music for giving thanks for a victory.

All this music belongs to the traditional church music of Western Christendom and it is known as *Gregorian chant*. We can still hear it live to-day in some churches and abbeys and there are also many excellent gramophone records produced by modern cantors. We can listen to the cantors of Solesmes in France, Einsiedeln in Switzerland, Montserrat and Silos in Spain, or to the female cantors of Argentan in Normandy or St Cecilia's Abbey on the Isle of Wight.

The name *Gregorian chant* most probably comes from St Gregory the Great, who was Pope from 590 until his death in 604. It was he who sent a group of monks as missionaries to England in 596 under the leadership of Augustine who became archbishop of Canterbury. One of the first things Augustine did was to found song schools so that English boys and young men could be trained as cantors. It is unlikely that St Gregory himself ever composed any chant and its origins certainly go back very much earlier than the sixth century: it undoubtedly predates Christianity by many centuries and its roots are to be found in that ancient semitic musical tradition passed on orally from one generation to the next.

The Jewish practice of chanting aloud the books of the Bible was carried over into the worship of the early Christian Church by Jewish cantors who had become Christians. Indeed, many melodies of the Jewish tradition can still be detected in the chant as we know it to-day. These melodies were adapted and added to until finally a specifically Christian and Western chant developed, using a Latin version of the sacred texts. It became a highly-wrought art of great beauty and perfection in its own right and it flourished with particular richness and creativity between the fifth and the ninth centuries, the period during which the basic repertoire was firmly established. Various chant 'dialects' — Old Roman, Gallican, etc., — were finally fused into 'Gregorian', which became the official chant throughout the Frankish Empire and is still with us to-day. The number of individual chants has been greatly increased since that time by the constant addition of new compositions. Each century has added to the repertoire something of its own and new pieces of chant are still being composed in our own day.

Notation

Gregorian chant is written in a special kind of musical notation using square notes and a four-lined stave. This square notation is based on that found in manuscripts of the thirteenth and fourteenth centuries (see page 28) which in its turn was derived from the earlier neum notation of the tenth century (see page 22). These two earlier forms of musical notation have certain advantages over modern staff notation. For instance often they show, by a single sign, how a number of notes may be grouped for a single syllable. Thus, the actual *visual effect* of the notation can assist the singer in an immediate grasp of the shape of the phrase and its structure, as, for example, in this passage:

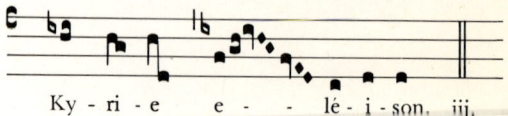

Shape and structure are less obvious in later forms of notation. The earlier notations, too, have ways of showing details of pronunciation and vocal interpretation for which no specific equivalents exist in modern staff notation. For these reasons the *traditional square notation* has been adopted throughout this book. Most singers seem to find it easier to read than modern staff notation. For one thing, they do not have to bother about the complexities of key signatures and time signatures.

A few simple explanations are offered here to help anyone who has not come across this notation before.

In the manuscripts three basic note shapes appear in various combinations. The first one originally represented a high note and was written as a rising stroke / in imitation of the movement of the choir-master raising his hand to show the rising melody.

This stroke was later stylized into the following shape ♩
The other two note shapes originally represented low notes and appeared in the manuscripts as - or .

These shapes developed into ■ or ♦

This last shape was normally reserved for a series of descending notes ♦♦ and arose from the angle at which the scribe held his pen.

In modern editions of Gregorian chant a single note sung to one syllable is usually written as a small black square ■

Using only single notes, this is how a Bishop might greet his people in Gregorian chant:

Pax vo - bis (Peace be with you)

This could be written in modern notation as:

Pax vo - bis

(See page 9 for use of this clef.)
And the people would reply:

Et cum spi - ri - tu tu - o
(And with thy spirit)

Et cum spi - ri - tu tu - o

Notice that a four-lined stave is used rather than a five-lined stave as in modern music. This is because many Gregorian melodies lie within a small compass, that of an average human voice. The little sign ⊏ is the DOH clef. The modern C clef 𝄡 used by viola players and showing middle C has developed from this clef

but, unlike the modern clef, the pitch it shows is relative, not absolute, and may be chosen to suit the range of the voices.

The other clef used in Gregorian chant is the FAH clef ⊏ from which the modern F or bass clef 𝄢 has developed. The FAH clef also shows relative, not absolute, pitch. It is interesting to note that the clef signs ⊏ and ⊏ arose out of the singer's need to be reminded of the position of the semitones in the diatonic scale, occurring between the warning clef line and the space immediately beneath: DOH–TE and FAH–ME. In the early manuscripts the line for DOH was sometimes coloured in yellow, or occasionally in green, and the FAH line was traced in red, an added visual reminder.

To choose a suitable pitch for a piece of chant, look for the highest and the lowest notes and decide at what pitch these can be sung most comfortably by the majority of the singers. Then see where these notes are placed in relation to the DOH and the FAH in order to get the semitones in the right places. For instance, chant No. 3 could be conveniently sung in the modern key of B♭ (B♭ = DOH). This would give the singers no note higher than C (RAY) in the psalm verses and no note lower than E♭ (FAH) in the antiphon. The psalm would be mainly recited on B♭, which is a good central reciting note. The opening phrase could be written in modern staff notation as follows:

A suitable pitch has been suggested for every piece in the collection.

The guide

Square notation has one excellent feature not to be found in modern staff notation: at the end of each stave line there is a small sign called a *guide* ♩ that shows you the pitch of the first note of the next stave line

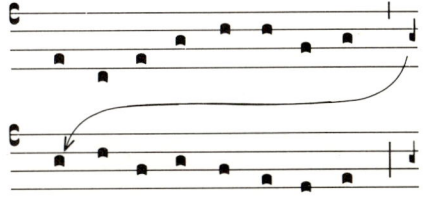

a great help in sight-reading at speed!

The flat

Only one accidental occurs in Gregorian chant, the flattened seventh degree: TAW instead of TE. You will find an example of this ♭ in No. 8 Kyrie *Orbis factor*.

Special forms: quilisma and liquescent

The quilisma is written thus and is explained in the notes to chant No. 2 (see page 12). For the liquescent see the notes to chant No. 5.

How length is shown

In some modern editions the obvious places where lengthening may be assumed, such as cadences, and some other less obvious ones, are marked by adding a dot to the note: ■· . This reminds the singer to double its duration, approximately. These somewhat ambiguous editorial signs have, however, been avoided and the details of interpretation left to each conductor. Read the paragraphs of *Duration* and *Phrasing* below for some simple guide-lines on how to sing with flexibility and good sense.

Duration

The time-value of an individual note is roughly the duration of a single short syllable in ordinary speech, but there is room for much flexibility: the earliest manuscripts with notation show the existence of both *a diminished and an augmented basic note-value*, as well as the normal one. Thus we can assume that there was not a rigidly fixed time-value. The chant is sung in a light and flowing way. One's best guide for this flexibility of note-duration is the Latin (or English) text itself and the manner in which it would be read aloud in a natural and lively fashion. (See also the hints on pronunciation and accent below, on page 8)

Repercussion

Doubling, or even tripling, of duration is traditionally shown by the addition of a second or a third note at the same pitch: ■■ or ■■■ . Each note, however, is separately sounded with very gentle repercussion:

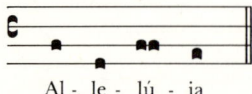

Al - le - lú - ia

A possible way of indicating this in modern notation would be:

Al - le - lú - ia

(See also comments on Nos. 9 and 17.)

The earliest manuscripts give many indications of subtle lengthenings and some of these will be discussed in the pages that follow. But many pieces of chant use only the simple notation described so far. Try singing the Nos. 1 and 11. If you find the rhythm difficult, read the words aloud as naturally and flowingly as possible, so as to bring out their meaning. It is sometimes a good plan to practise whispering the words, because this makes one aware of the ACCENTS. When the finest chants were being composed the Latin language was already evolving into a romance language with a principal (tonic) accent on every word. This accent was of its nature light, resilient and usually high-pitched. So try to read the Latin with a lilting 'Italian' pronunciation. In the English version the rhythms are more familiar. Listen to the natural speech-rhythms of the words. Then sing through the melody, perhaps using solfa to accustom yourself to interpreting the four-lined stave. Now sing the melody with its own words, trying to feel how the rhythm emerges flexibly.

Phrasing

There are no regularly recurring bar-lines in the chant, because the rhythm is free. In this book phrasing has been shown by the use of the

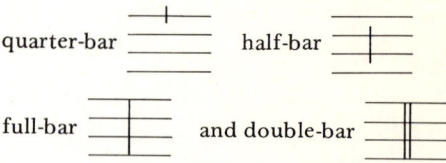

quarter-bar   half-bar

full-bar   and double-bar

These are a form of musical punctuation: the quarter-bar is rather like a comma, the half-bar is like a semicolon or a colon, and the full-bar is like a full-stop. The double-bar corresponds to the end of the paragraph. In the following examples approximate lengthening based on phrasing has been shown in the transcriptions into modern notation.

Two notes for one syllable: High—Low and Low—High

The manuscripts also give signs showing when two notes are sung to one syllable. The gesture of the conductor's hand was closely imitated by the pen of the scribe: a high note followed by a low note was written ⌐ or ⌐ . By the fourteenth century this sign had developed into

Je - su   Chri - ste

This could be written in modern notation:

Je - su   Chri - ste

A low note followed by a high note was written ∕ or ✓ This sign became ♪

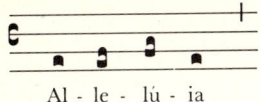
Al - le - lú - ia

In modern notation this might be written as follows:

Al - le - lú - ia

Nos. 3 and 16 give practice in this.

Three notes for one syllable

	Early manuscripts	Square notation	Example	Modern notation
High—Low—Lower			Cho - rus	Cho - rus
Low—High—Higher			Je - sum Chri - stum	Je - sum Chri - stum
Low—High—Low			A - men	A - men
High—Low—High			A - men	A - men

Al - le - lú - ia   Al - le - lú - ia

No. 7 and the Amens above give practice in these groups

Four or more notes to one syllable

All these basic note-groups may be further developed by the addition of extra notes, for example:

Pa - tris
Sal - ve

Pa - tris
Sal - ve

Now try singing No. 10, the *Easter Alleluias*.

7

A word about modality

None of the pieces in this collection is composed in the familiar major and minor modes of later music, which can be recognized by having as their tonic (or 'home-note') the DOH or the LAH. Instead, the melodies gravitate around other notes of the scale and this contributes to their extraordinary richness and variety. The tonic, or 'home-note', will be found to be RAY, ME, FAH, or SOH. Look at the *last note* of each piece to see whether it is in the RAY mode (PROTUS), or the ME mode (DEUTERUS), the FAH mode (TRITUS), or the SOH mode (TETRARDUS). Medieval musical theory further subdivided these four families into Modes I and II (RAY), III and IV (ME), V and VI (FAH), and VII and VIII (SOH), according to the range and to the choice of reciting notes. But the modes are perhaps more truly to be recognized by characteristic phrases, particularly intonations and cadences — beginnings and endings.

The words

Guide to the pronunciation of the Latin

Modern Italian is the living language which most nearly approaches, in character and pronunciation, the Latin spoken at the time the chant was being composed. So the following guidelines may be helpful. Use pure Italian vowels. A near approximation in English is as follows:

Vowels	a	as in FATHER
	e	as in MET, but approaching the sound of MATE
	i	as the double EE in MEET
	o	as the exclamation OH, but avoiding the English diphthong
	u	as the double OO in MOON
Diphthong	æ	as in MET (see above)
Consonants	c	hard, as in CAT, before A, O, U
	c	soft, pronounced like English CH, as in CHICHESTER, before E, I
	g	hard, as in GAME, before A, O, U
	g	soft, as in GINGER, before E, I
	gn	pronounced NY, e.g. 'MAGNUS' = 'MANYUS'
	gu	pronounced GW before a vowel, e.g. 'LINGUA' = 'LINGWA'
	h	always silent, but pronounced hard, like a K, in these two words: 'MIHI', 'NIHIL', which used to be spelt 'michi', 'nichil'
	qu	pronounced KW, e.g. 'QUOD' is pronounced 'KWOD'
	ti	before another vowel is pronounced TSI, e.g. 'REVELATIONEM GENTIUM' is pronounced 'REVELATSIONEM GENTSIUM'. In all other cases the 't' is pronounced as in English
	xc	the C is softened after X to 'SH', e.g. in the word 'EXCELSIS' the sound approximates that of 'EGGSHELLS'

The Latin accent

In words of *two syllables* the tonic accent occurs on the first syllable. As this is always the case it has not seemed necessary to mark the place of this accent. But in words of three or more syllables the tonic accent may occur on the last syllable but one or the last but two. So the place of the accent has been clearly marked in these words, as follows:

di-úr-nis ác-ti-bus

Using English words

The chant has grown out of the Latin text and is most perfect musically when sung to Latin words. It is quite possible, however, to sing it in other languages, including English. The new English translations used in this book have been made with one aim in view: that they should be singable without alteration to the original melody. A few existing translations of high quality have been included where, as a general rule, they respect the Latin word-setting. Passages from the *Book of Common Prayer* and other sources have also been used, sometimes with slight modification to fit them to existing chants. All English singing versions retain as far as possible the material and spirit of the original texts. In a few of the very well-known texts, such as the *Gloria Patri* (Glory be) where there are more syllables in English than in Latin, the text has not been changed, but void square notes have been provided for the extra syllables, as follows:

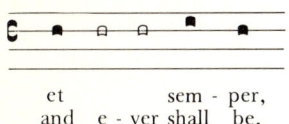

et   sem - per,
and   e - ver shall   be,

Use of high and low voices

In the preceding examples using modern staff notation the G clef with a small figure 8 has been used: indicating pitch one octave below the treble clef; and once the F or bass clef: . This would suggest that the chant was meant to be sung by men's voices alone, basses and baritones. But the chant is for everybody, men, women and young people, not only for choirs of monks. It can be sung by high or low voices, or by both in unison or in alternation.

The tradition of female choirs singing the chant is extremely ancient. St Jerome (fourth century) tells us that one of his pupils, Blesilla, outshone all her companions in singing the *Alleluia*. In the early Church, choirs of celibates, men and women, appear to have sung the psalms antiphonally during the services. And the pilgrim Egeria, in the fourth century, tells of choirs of children, in Jerusalem, who used to reply 'Kyrie eleison' to the deacon's petitions. In the medieval instructions on how to sing the services in Salisbury Cathedral, there were certain chants that were reserved for the boy choristers with their treble voices, and others for the adult members of the choir. And to-day, in houses of Benedictine nuns, the chant is naturally sung by high voices alone, as it has been since the time of St Scholastica, the sister of St Benedict (sixth century).

If you have both high and low voices in your choir, it would sound better for them to take turns in singing rather than to sing together in octaves all the time. For example, in the hymns the first verse might be sung by the low voices and the second by the high voices, and so on. Both high and low voices might join forces for the final verse and the *Amen*. It also sounds very well if you arrange to alternate between a solo singer and a group. Or you could have two cantors singing the solo parts. On solemn feasts it is customary to increase the number of cantors to three or four. The places where alternation is essential have been marked in the text.

The use of instruments

The chant is best sung with no instrumental accompaniment at all: it is quite complete in itself and was originally never intended to have any accompaniment. Yet the chant may be said to have been responsible for the development of most of our Western musical heritage, including a great deal of music composed for instruments as well as voices. A notable part of the music composed between the fourteenth and the seventeenth centuries, for example, was written to be performed in alternation with sections of the chant: *alternatim*, as it was called. A short contrapuntal passage played on the organ or sung by a polyphonic choir would be followed by a phrase or two of chant, and so on to the end of the piece. If you ever feel like experimenting with *alternatim* music, the Tallis hymns, for example, or Couperin's *Messe pour les paroisses*, remember that the chant itself will have to be slowed down considerably and its style adapted to that of the sections of organ music or polyphony, which often have one note of the chant equivalent to one whole bar of the music. For there have been different ways of interpreting the chant in different centuries, and in the sixteenth and seventeenth centuries it was sung in an extremely slow and stately way.

At the time of the Renaissance secular instrumental music was sometimes composed around a plainchant theme, such as the numerous instrumental *In Nomine*'s constructed upon the first antiphon of Vespers for Trinity Sunday, *Gloria tibi Trinitas*, a particularly popular chant melody. You will find this antiphon in No. 23 and you can play it on a recorder or violin.

But above all, try to discover the chant by *singing* as much of it as you can, without any instruments to distract your attention from its own very special flavour. Try to hear it and enjoy it in its own right, and then you will be able to appreciate to the full its variety, strength, beauty and delicacy. Try to sing it in the spirit and at the tempo at which it was originally intended to be sung and from the delicacy of the neum notation it appears that it must have been very light and fast and flowing.

If this is your first taste of the chant you may find it strange at first, but do go on until it becomes quite familiar. There are many delights in store: may this small collection be an invitation to explore even further the inestimable treasures of the chant repertoire!

Music round the year

'Sweetly sang the monks in Ely
  When King Canute rowed by:
"Row, men, nearer the land,
  And let us hear this song of the monks."'

Translated from the Latin (Trinity College, Cambridge, MS 0.2.1., fo. 70v)

The Church's year begins with Advent, and proceeds through Christmas to Lent. Passiontide and Easter. Then follow Ascensiontide, Whitsuntide, Trinity Sunday and all the remaining Sundays of the year till Advent comes round again.

Seasonal pieces can be sung as living liturgy during religious services, or at school assemblies at the appropriate time of the year. They can be used as part of a ceremony of carols, with drama or mime depicting the events of the Gospel story. Some of the pieces in this section are particularly suitable for processions: the music was often sung in this way during the Middle Ages. An interesting historical experience could be reconstructed. Processions could also be incorporated as part of the background of a history play. The Candlemas procession could be enacted as if by the monks in an abbey church, or the clergy in a cathedral choir. The singers might also represent a medieval crowd of pilgrims taking part in an outdoor procession of the Cross: the *Vexilla regis* (No. 4) would be suitable for this.

Nuns in procession

1 An Advent hymn *Conditor alme siderum*

Suggested pitch
Take DOH (here the top line) to be top E♭,
so that the first note will be the G
above middle C.

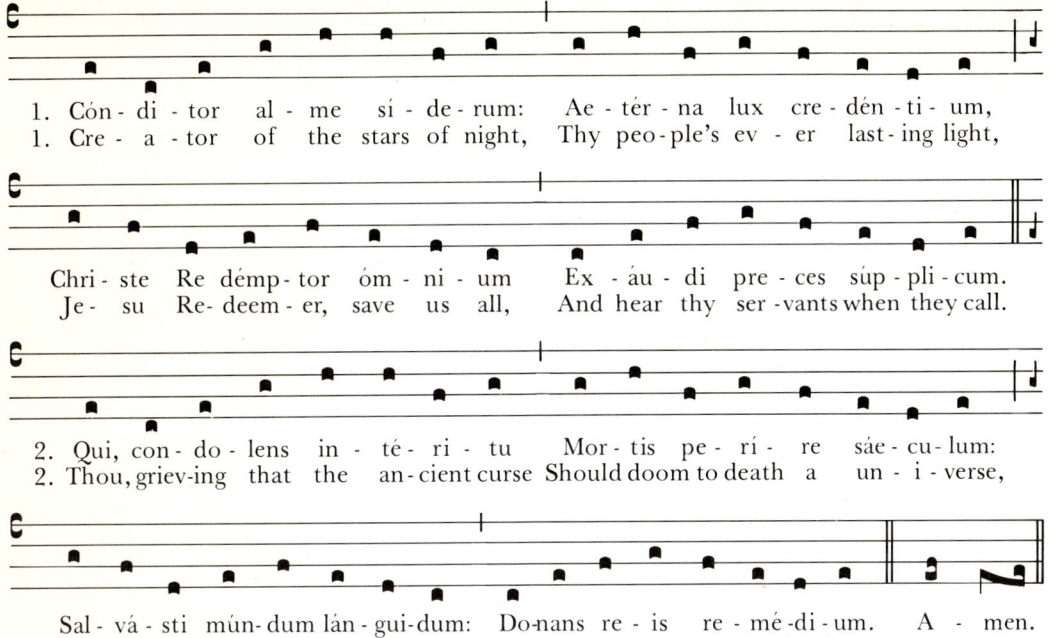

1. Cón-di-tor al-me sí-de-rum: Ae-tér-na lux cre-dén-ti-um,
1. Cre-a-tor of the stars of night, Thy peo-ple's ev-er last-ing light,

Chri-ste Redémp-tor óm-ni-um Ex-áu-di pre-ces súp-pli-cum.
Je-su Re-deem-er, save us all, And hear thy ser-vants when they call.

2. Qui, con-do-lens in-té-ri-tu Mor-tis pe-rí-re sáe-cu-lum:
2. Thou, griev-ing that the an-cient curse Should doom to death a un-i-verse,

Sal-vá-sti mún-dum lán-gui-dum: Do-nans re-is re-mé-di-um. A-men.
Hast found the medi-cine full of grace, To save and heal a ru-ined race. A-men.

3 Vergénte mundi véspere
  Uti sponsus de thálamo
  Egréssus honestissima
  Vírginis Matris cláusula.

4 Cujus forti poténtiae
  Genu curvántur ómnia
  Caeléstia, terréstria,
  Faténtur nutu subdita.

5 Te deprecámur Ágie,
  Ventúre Judex sáeculi,
  Consérva nos in témpore
  Hostis a telo pérfidi.

6 Laus honor virtus glória
  Deo Patri et Fílio
  Sancto simul Paráclito
  In sempitérna sáecula. Amen.

3 Thou cam'st, the Bridegroom of the bride,
  As drew the world to evening-tide;
  Proceeding from a virgin shrine,
  The spotless Victim all divine:

4 At whose dread name, majestic now,
  All knees must bend, all hearts must bow;
  And things celestial thee shall own,
  And things terrestrial, Lord alone.

5 O thou whose coming is with dread
  To judge and doom the quick and dead,
  Preserve us, while we dwell below,
  From every insult of the foe.

6 To God the Father, God the Son,
  And God the Spirit, Three in One,
  Laud, honour, might, and glory be
  From age to age eternally. Amen.

A hymn is a poem sung in praise of God. Many hymns are written in strict poetic metres, such as iambic tetrameter. They may be built up of several *strophes* (or verses), each one having four lines, or six lines, etc. Strophic hymns form a special category of their own — quite different from the rest of the chant repertoire. They were introduced from Syria in the fourth century and are often associated with the name of St Ambrose, who was Bishop of Milan.

This is a well-known Advent Office hymn for an evening service, dating from the seventh century. (You can read about the daily office on page 23.) During the later Middle Ages this popular hymn tune was sometimes sung in a swinging triple measure:

and you can try singing it like that, if you like: it is almost impossible to sing it 'straight', as a succession of equal notes, though some cantors do perform it that way! Try both ways, and see which comes more naturally and which you prefer.

2   A Christmas antiphon *Hodie Christus*

There are a number of antiphons (or short refrains) that begin with the word 'Hodie' (On this day). This antiphon, sung before and after the *Magnificat* during Second Vespers (Evensong) on Christmas Day, may already be familiar to you, for an English version of the tune was used by Benjamin Britten as a *Processional* and *Recessional* in his well-known *Ceremony of Carols*. For many people this has been their first introduction to the chant.

The antiphon contains one odd-looking group of notes: (High—low—high—higher), that needs some elucidation. Note that the group occurs on the principal syllable of two important words, 'Christus' and 'exsúltant'. Now look at the third note, which is a little saw-edged sign called a *quilisma*. This sign always leads upwards, and generally to a note that is a semitone higher, as here. It should be sung lightly, since it is only leading towards the note of arrival (here the flattened note). The two notes that precede the quilisma are sung rather broadly and almost doubled in length. The group might be written as follows in modern notation, though do remember that transcriptions are only an approximation to the truth:

When you have sung this splendid antiphon, compare it with Benjamin Britten's version.

3 A processional chant for Candlemas *Lumen*

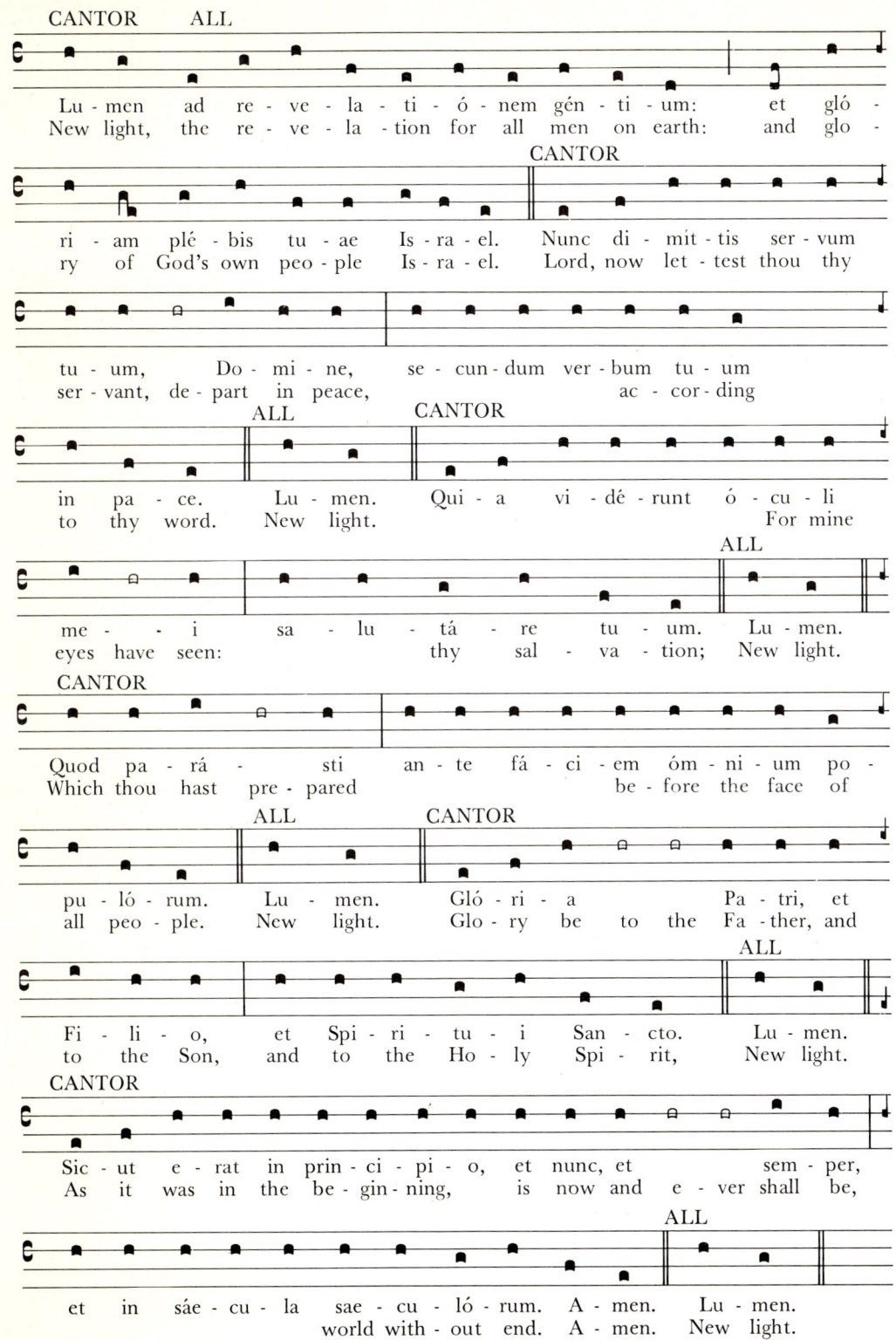

13

The day when the Infant Jesus was presented in the Temple by his parents in obedience to the Law of Moses (Luke 2: 22–39) has been celebrated ever since the fourth century. Each year, on 2 February, candles are blessed and distributed to everyone and then carried alight in procession. The words of the chant proclaim Christ, the Light of the World. They were first uttered by old Simeon as he received the child in his arms and gave glory to God. One or two cantors begin by singing the word 'Lumen'. Everyone else joins in at 'ad revelationem gentium'. Notice the careful balance of the two phrases of the refrain. The cantors sing the verses of the *Nunc dimittis* and everyone takes up the refrain between the verses.

How to make a procession

A wealth of detail exists to tell us about the processions that used to take place in Salisbury Cathedral during the Middle Ages. There used to be a procession every Sunday and every Feast Day. A typical procession would be headed by a verger to keep back the crowds and clear the way for the clergy. Behind him came a boy in a surplice carrying a bucket of holy water. Then came an acolyte wearing an alb, carrying the processional cross. Sometimes there were as many as three processional crosses. Two candle-bearers followed, also in albs. Behind these came the thurifers, swinging their censers. Then the Subdeacon and Deacon, in dalmatic and tunicle, and the Priest in a silk cope. Then came the choristers, all wearing silk copes, and the rest of the clergy, also in copes; and finally the Bishop wearing his mitre and carrying his crozier. On some occasions banners were carried at the head of the procession, first one depicting a lion, then various others, and behind them all a banner in the shape of a dragon. Reliquaries might also be carried.

The first picture shows the positions of some of those taking part in the Candlemas procession as they stood for the blessing of the candles. The second picture shows the banners and reliquary that were carried during the Ascension Day procession.

Candlemas procession

Ascension Day procession

4 A hymn for the cross *Vexilla regis*

DOH = D
First note G

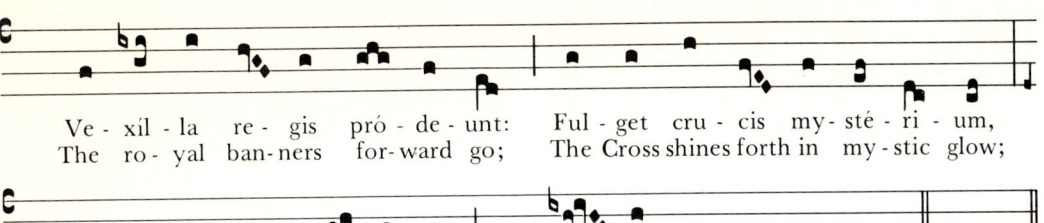

Ve - xil - la re - gis pró - de - unt: Ful - get cru - cis my - sté - ri - um,
The ro - yal ban - ners for-ward go; The Cross shines forth in my-stic glow;

Quo car - ne car - nis Cón - di - tor Sus - pén - sus est pa - tí - bu - lo. A - men.
Where he in flesh, our flesh who made, Our sen -tence bore, our ran-som paid: A - men.

2 Quo vulnerátus ínsuper
  Mucróne dirae lánceae:
  Ut nos laváret crímine
  Manávit unda sánguine.

3 Impléta sunt quae cóncinit
  David fidélis cármine,
  Dicéndo natiónibus
  Regnávit a ligno Deus.

4 Arbor decóra et fúlgida
  Ornáta regis púrpura,
  Elécta digno stípite
  Tam sancta membra tángere.

5 Beáta cujus bráchiis
  Précium pepéndit sáeculi:
  Statéra facta est córporis
  Praedámque tulit tártaris.

6 O crux ave spes única
  Hoc passiónis témpore,
  Auge piis justíciam
  Reísque dona véniam.

7 Te summa Deus Trínitas
  Colláudet omnis spíritus:
  Quos per crucis mystérium
  Salvas, rege per sáecula. Amen.

2 Where deep for us the spear was dyed,
  Life's torrent rushing from his side,
  To wash us in that precious flood,
  Where mingled Water flowed, and Blood.

3 Fulfilled is all that David told
  In true prophetic song of old;
  Amidst the nations, God, saith he,
  Hath reigned and triumphed from the tree.

4 O Tree of beauty, Tree of light!
  O Tree with royal purple dight!
  Elect on whose triumphal breast
  Those holy limbs should find their rest:

5 On whose dear arms, so widely flung,
  The weight of this world's ransom hung:
  The price of humankind to pay,
  And spoil the spoiler of his prey.

6 O Cross, our one reliance, hail!
  So may thy power with us avail
  To give new virtue to the saint,
  And pardon to the penitent.

7 To thee, eternal Three in One,
  Let homage meet by all be done:
  Whom by the Cross thou dost restore,
  Preserve and govern evermore. Amen.

The Latin poet Venantius Fortunatus, Bishop of Poitiers and a contemporary of St Gregory the Great, was the author of this fine poem on the Cross. We do not know whether he, too, composed the magnificent melody that has come down to us. This is the version of it that would have been sung all over England in past centuries during Passiontide, the preparation for Easter when Christ's death and resurrection are celebrated. The melody is very different in style from the lilting, syllabic tune of *Conditor alme siderum*: it is grave and solemn, rather majestic in tone. Try not to hurry the groups of two or three notes to one syllable. The last line even has one group of five notes to a single syllable, and this group needs to be sung quite boldly, with a fine legato. You should not have any difficulty in working out the notes:  (low–high–higher–low–lower). Give the groups plenty of breadth, and sing the whole hymn with a great sense of spaciousness.

If you sing the other verses with their original Latin words, notice that there are several cases of elision. In verse 4, for example, you run together the final 'a' of 'decora' and the 'e' of 'et', so that it sounds like 'decoret'. And in verse 5 the word 'precium' has to be sung as two, not three syllables. And in the third line of the same verse you run together 'facta' and 'est', so that it sounds like 'factest'.

5 An Easter responsory *Surrexit Dominus*

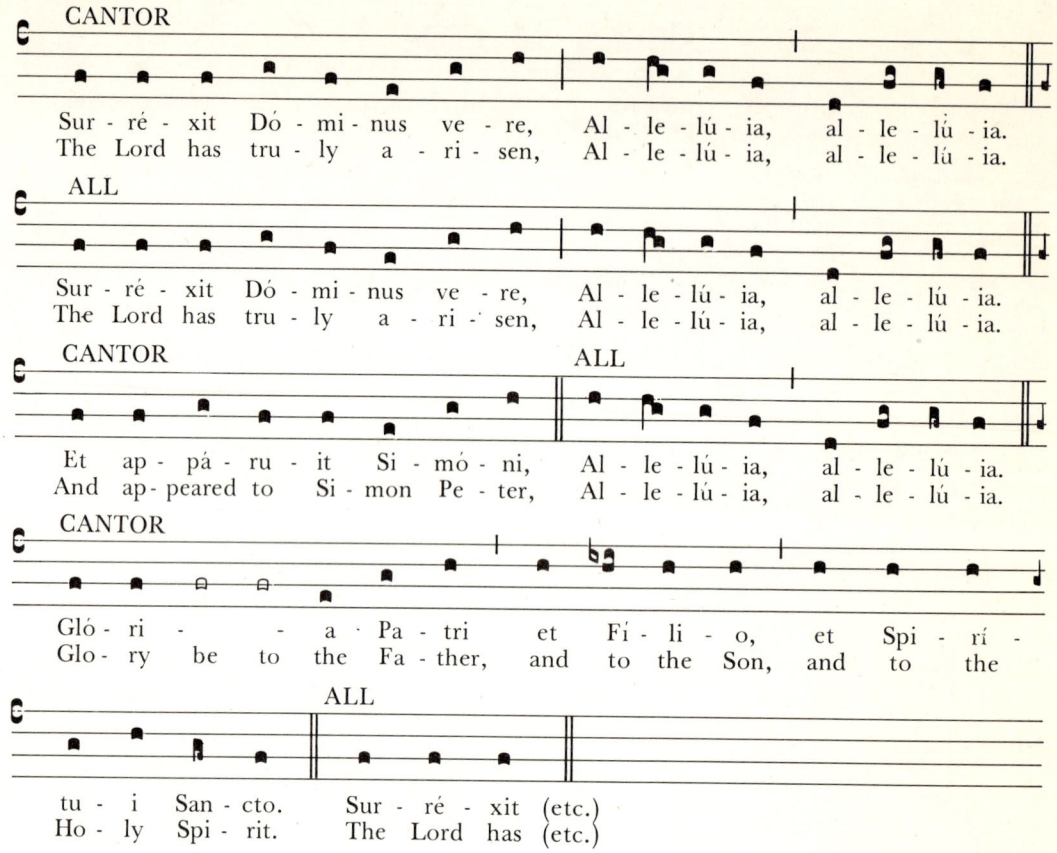

Responsories are special chants that are sung after the Scripture readings. Some are quite simple, like this short Easter one. Others are very elaborate pieces, intended for performance by very experienced solo cantors. This responsory could be sung after a reading of one of the Gospel accounts of the risen Christ (see No. 17 for Readings).

Responsories are rather like a miniature rondo in form. The cantor gives the lead, singing

'Surréxit Dóminus vere, Allelúia, allelúia.'
Everyone repeats this. Then the cantor sings the verse

'Et appáruit Simóni,'
and everyone repeats the *second half* of the original phrase, the alleluias.
Then the cantor sings another verse:
    'Glória Patri . . . ' (etc.)
and everyone repeats the original phrase
    'Surréxit Dóminus vere, Allelúia, allelúia.'

Notice the curious little note in the second line that looks like a misprint ♮ This is called a *liquescent*, and it is there to remind you to sing very carefully the smooth change from the 'u' vowel sound through the 'i' to the final 'a'. Liquescents are often used for notating the way to sing an 'l' an 'm' or an 'n', etc., as these consonants are partially vocalized (or hummed) and are sung rather quietly — hence the half-sized note. There are some more examples of liquescents in Nos. 10, 14, 17, etc.

6 Two Easter versicles

DOH = C
First note C

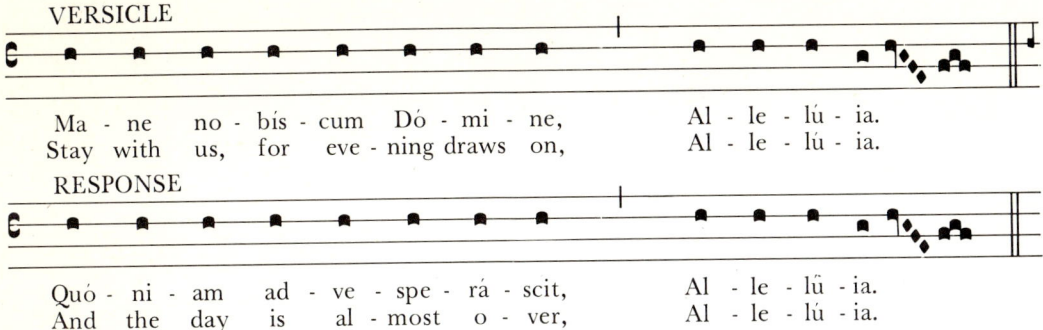

DOH = C
First note C

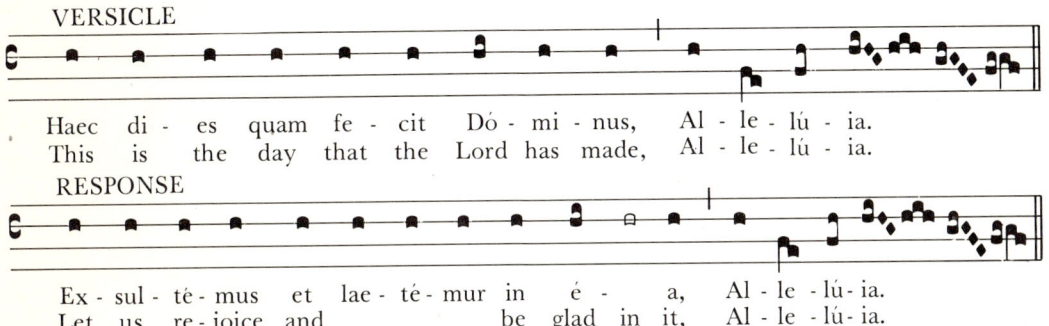

Versicles and responses are tiny conversations in chant. Notice that both versicle and response have the same music. The cantor sings the versicle and everyone replies. So both the soloist and the group have the chance of enjoying the lively, decorative flourish at the end. In the first example, pause slightly on the first note of the last syllable before launching into this flourish:

and in the *Haec dies*, lengthen the DOH before the final descent, as follows:

A versicle and response may be sung between a psalm and a reading, after a final antiphon, or a hymn, or before a prayer.

You might like to mime the story told at the end of St Luke's Gospel (Luke 24: 13–35), the story of the Disciples of Emmaus, and to sing the versicle *Mane nobiscum Domine* (etc.) as the disciples reach the inn and Jesus pretends he is going further on. Or you could sing the words of the passage from Luke to a reading tone (see No. 18) and add the versicle at the end. Or a solo cantor could recite the passage from St Mark's Gospel (Mark 16: 1–8) which tells of the events of the first Easter morning, the finding of the empty tomb. The choir could then add the versicle *Haec dies* (etc.).

7 A hymn to the Holy Spirit *Veni creator*

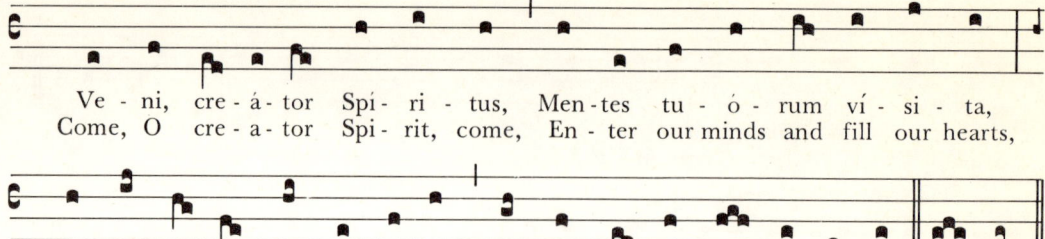

Ve - ni, cre - á - tor Spi - ri - tus, Men - tes tu - ó - rum ví - si - ta,
Come, O cre - a - tor Spi - rit, come, En - ter our minds and fill our hearts,

Im - ple su - pér - na grá - ti - a Quae tu cre - á - sti, péc - to - ra. A-men.
Im - plant in us grace from a - bove: May your creatures show forth your love. A-men.

2 Qui díceris Paráclitus,
   Donum Dei altissimi,
   Fons vivus, ignis, cáritas
   Et spiritális únctio.

3 Tu septifórmis múnere,
   Dextrae Dei tu digitus,
   Tu rite promissum Patris,
   Sermóne ditans gúttura.

4 Accende lumen sénsibus,
   Infúnde amorem córdibus,
   Infírma nostri córporis
   Virtúte firmans pérpeti.

5 Hostem repéllas lóngius
   Pacémque dones prótinus:
   Ductóre sic te práevio
   Vitémus omne nóxium.

6 Per te sciámus da Patrem
   Noscámus atque Fílium,
   Te utriúsque Spíritum
   Credámus omni témpore. Amen.

2 Past ages called you Paraclete,
   Gift to mankind of God most high,
   Well-spring of life, fire, charity,
   And anointing Spirit of peace.

3 You bring to men your seven gifts,
   You are the power of God's right hand,
   The Promise of God to the Church,
   Words of life upon lips of men.

4 Illumine all our hearts anew,
   And pour your love into our souls,
   Refresh our weak frame with new strength,
   Fortitude, and grace to endure.

5 Cast far away our deadly foe,
   Grant us your peace for evermore:
   With you as our guide on the way
   Evil shall no more harm our souls.

6 Teach us the Trinity to know,
   In Father, Son, and Spirit, One:
   The Three in One and One in Three,
   Now and ever, eternally. Amen.

One of the best known and most loved hymns of the Western Church. In England this famous tune used to be associated with a Christmas hymn, *Salvator mundi*, of which many sixteenth-century settings exist. The tune has that rare quality of ease and apparent inevitability, yet its four phrases are as artistically and cunningly constructed as the lines of a sonnet, rising to a climax in the third phrase and sinking gently down with gracefully balanced patterning to a final cadence on SOH.

This hymn to the Holy Spirit is sung at the beginning of any important religious ceremony, such as the consecration of a bishop, the coronation service for a reigning monarch, or the ordination of a priest. During the Council of Constance (1414–18) there was a daily procession and prayers were offered for the election of a new Pope to end the chaos of the Great Schism. The procession was made up of all the members of the Council and all the clergy of the city and it included two hundred choristers clothed in their white surplices. As they processed everyone chanted the *Veni Creator*. On 11 November 1417, the future Pope Martin V was elected. Cardinal Fillastre wrote in his diary:

'They marched every day past the front of the Conclave hall, singing the *Veni Creator* so devoutly that many in the Conclave wept to hear it and could not restrain their tears. The innocent children of the city sang in their high voices with the clergy, sounding full of earnestness. They were clearly and plainly heard from the Conclave ... The electors were praying on their knees and many were stirred to tears.'

The languages of the chant

I Greek

8 Kyrie *Orbis factor*

The chant has not always been sung in Latin. One of the first languages used by the early Christians was Greek, and the words Kyrie eleison, Christe eleison (Lord have mercy, Christ have mercy) are still used to-day in both East and West. In the West the *Kyrie eleison* was once part of a longer chant, sung before the service began to allow a little extra time for the late-comers! This setting is traditionally sung at Mass on ordinary Sundays throughout the year. It is called 'Kyrie Orbis factor' (Lord, Creator of the World) because extra words used sometimes to be inserted between 'Kyrie' and 'eleison', fitting the syllables to the flow of notes. These words were often a meditation upon the mystery of the Trinity. Each invocation is sung three times, so that there are nine invocations in all.

This chant could be sung by two groups of singers in alternation. The first Kyrie might be intoned by a solo singer and continued by the first choir from the asterisk. Choir 2 could sing the second Kyrie, Choir 1 the third, Choir 2 the first Christe, and so on. In the final Kyrie both choirs could sing together from the asterisk to the end.

When interpreting the rhythm, slow up the first two notes of the last syllable 'e' of each Kyrie and also the high first note of the syllable 'ste' of Christe. Then let the melody flow on, unhurriedly, towards the cadence of each phrase.

'Kyrie eleison' is pronounced 'KEE-REE-AY E-LAY-EE-SONN', as if it were Latin.

Cantors in choir

II Greek and Latin

9 The Trisagion from the Good Friday Liturgy

Sometimes both Greek and Latin were used together in the same services. A fourth-century Spanish nun, Egeria, who went on a pilgrimage to the Holy Land, describes bilingual and even trilingual practice in the church of Jerusalem.

'In this province there are some people who know both Greek and Syriac, but others know only one or the other. The bishop may know Syriac, but he never uses it. He always speaks in Greek, and has a presbyter beside him who translates the Greek into Syriac, so that everyone can understand what he means. Similarly the lessons read in church have to be read in Greek, but there is always someone in attendance to translate into Syriac so that the people understand. Of course there are also people here who speak neither Greek nor Syriac, but Latin. But there is no need for them to be discouraged, since some of the brothers or sisters who speak Latin as well as Greek will explain things to them.'

This piece is the solemn *Trisagion*, or 'Thrice Holy', from the Ceremony of the Cross on Good Friday. Two choirs answer each other, one in Greek and one in Latin. The pronunciation of the Greek is Latinized as follows:

Hagios	= Agios — three syllables — silent 'h', hard g
Theos	= Teos
Ischyros	= Ischiros — the ch like k
Athanatos	= Atánatos
hymas	= imas — silent 'h'

There are a few interesting points of singing technique in this chant. First of all, when two groups of notes follow one another at the same pitch the last note of the first group and the first note of the second should both be sounded with an individual, but rather gentle impulse, or 'repercussion' and not run together as one long note:

not

There are numerous examples of this elsewhere in the piece. Something similar occurs in the last two phrases, where an extra note is added at the end of a group and at the same pitch as the last note of it. This note, too, should be gently sounded as an individual note:

Finally, the group on the last syllable of 'Athanatos' and 'Immortalis' contains both a *quilisma* and a repercussion. (Look at the notes on the antiphon *Hodie* (No. 2) for an explanation of the *quilisma*.) In modern notation this phrase might be written approximately as follows:

This rich, rising phrase and the one that follows are two of the most famous and beautiful in the whole repertoire, and surprisingly easy to sing.

Note that in this piece the whole point of the two alternating choirs singing, one in Greek, and one in Latin, would be lost if the singing were in English rather than in the original languages. The English translation is only there this time to help you to understand the meaning and is not intended to be sung. So do not attempt to fit it to the music!

III *Hebrew*

10   Three Easter Alleluias

Lauds. Easter vigil

DOH = D
First note G

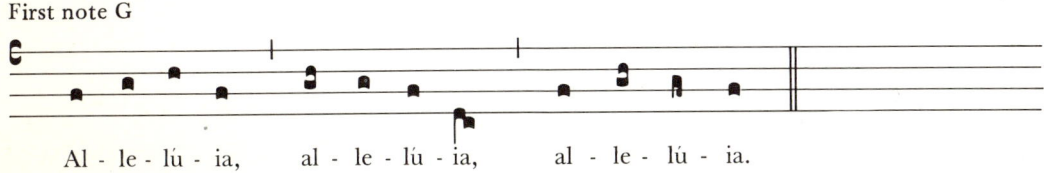

Lauds. Low Sunday

Whitsuntide

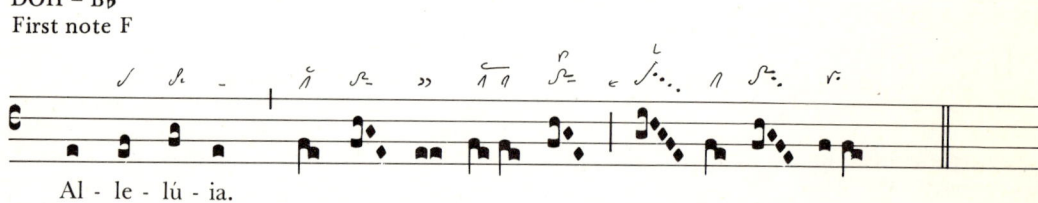

Besides Latin and Greek there are a number of Hebrew words in the chant, those most frequently found being *Amen* (so let it be) and *Alleluia* (praise God). The *Alleluia* is a shout of joy and praise and it is particularly characteristic of Eastertide.

These three examples demonstrate quite well the variety of ways in which this word can be set to music. The first is a straightforward antiphon, sung as a refrain to a psalm during the Easter Vigil. The little note that looks like a misprint (last but one of the piece) above the syllable 'ú' is a *liquescent* ♩ It should be sung very gently and smoothly as the vowel 'u' changes to 'i' for the last syllable.

The second example is a ninefold *alleluia* antiphon, sung at Lauds (Morning Prayer) on the Sunday after Easter. It should be sung quite fast, with lightness and verve.

The third example is a fully developed florid piece that used to be sung on the Saturday after Whit Sunday and also on Trinity Sunday. This particular Sunday was one of the days on which men who had finished their years of training were made priests at a special service of ordination. The music flows on above the syllable 'a' and this wordless vocalization is called a *Jubilus*. Some of the signs of the original neum notation have been added so that you can see the care with which the scribes worked. The little c's mean 'celeriter' (fast) and are an indication of light, quick singing. On the other hand, the horizontal signs before the quarter-bar and the half-bar tell the singer that he is to hold back slightly at these points.

Hours of the day and moments of life

'Seven times a day I praise thee'
(Psalm 119: 164)

11 A morning hymn *Jam lucis*

DOH = C
First note F

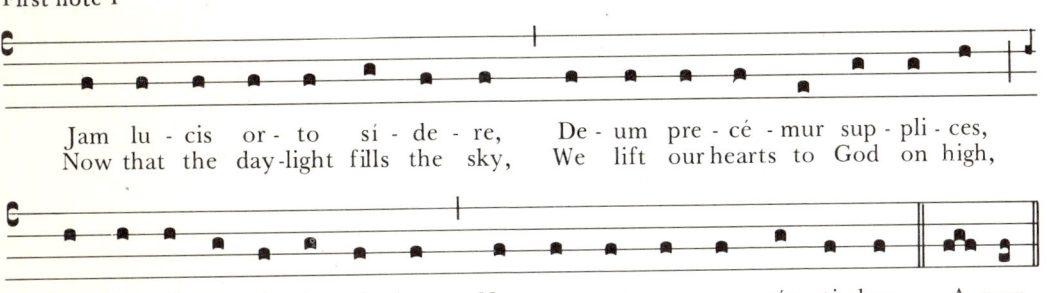

Jam lu-cis or-to si-de-re, De-um pre-cé-mur sup-pli-ces,
Now that the day-light fills the sky, We lift our hearts to God on high,

Ut in di-úr-nis ác-ti-bus Nos ser-vet a no-cén-ti-bus. A-men.
That he, in all we do or say, Would keep us free from harm to-day. A-men.

2 Linguam refrǽnans témperet,
  Ne litis horror ínsonet:
  Visum fovéndo cóntegat,
  Ne vanitates háuriat.

3 Sint pura cordis íntima,
  Absístat et vecórdia:
  Carnis terat supérbiam
  Potus cibíque párcitas.

4 Ut cum dies abscésserit,
  Noctémque sors redúxerit,
  Mundi per abstinéntiam
  Ipsi canámus glóriam.

5 Deo Patri sit glória,
  Ejúsque soli Fílio,
  Cum Spíritu Paráclito,
  Et nunc et in perpétuum. Amen.

2 Would guard our hearts and tongues from strife;
  From anger's din would hide our life;
  From all ill sights would turn our eyes;
  Would close our ears from vanities:

3 Would keep our inmost conscience pure;
  Our souls from folly would secure;
  Would bid us check the pride of sense
  With due and holy abstinence.

4 So we, when this new day is gone,
  And night in turn is drawing on,
  With conscience from the world unstained
  Shall praise his name for victory gained.

5 All laud to God the Father be;
  All praise, eternal Son, to thee;
  All glory, as is ever meet,
  To God the holy Paraclete. Amen.

'Seven times a day I praise thee'. We know from the accounts in the New Testament that the first Christians continued the practice of their Jewish forebears and sang the praises of God at regular intervals throughout the day (e.g. Acts 3: 1, 'One day at three in the afternoon, the hour of prayer, Peter and John were on their way to the Temple ... '). By the sixth century St Benedict had organized the day's prayer for his monks so that the seven services followed each other at roughly three-hourly intervals. This hymn comes from the Office of Prime, the first of the Little Hours of the Divine Office, sung traditionally at 6.00 a.m. The other Little Hours followed at

9.00 a.m. (Terce, or the Third Hour), midday (Sext, or the Sixth Hour) and 3.00 p.m. (None, or the Ninth Hour, from which our modern words 'noon' and 'afternoon' have been derived). The two Greater Hours are Lauds and Vespers, sung with greater solemnity than the Little Hours and marking the moments of sunrise and sunset. The final service of the day, which 'completes' the series and is therefore called 'Compline', is sung just before bed-time. All these services are made up of psalms and short readings and a hymn and they end with a 'collect' or prayer.

The high point of the monastic day is of course the Mass, usually celebrated after Terce, and forming a focus for all the Hours.

The night office or Office of Readings, is also known as 'Vigils', or 'Matins'. It used to be celebrated at midnight. The night office has longer readings and elaborate responsories.

To get the feeling of the medieval integration of prayer and daily life the occasional performance of the pieces in this chapter at the appropriate times would be an interesting experiment.

12 An evening hymn *Te lucis*

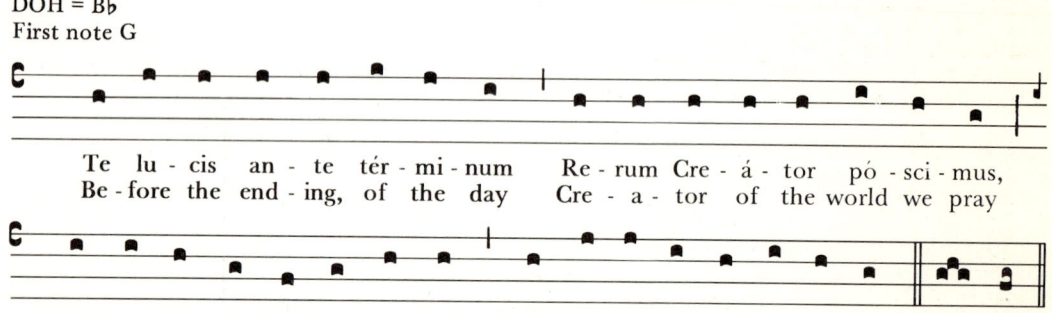

DOH = B♭
First note G

Te lu-cis an-te tér-mi-num   Re-rum Cre-á-tor pó-sci-mus,
Be-fore the end-ing, of the day   Cre-a-tor of the world we pray

Ut só-li-ta cle-mén-ti-a   Sis prae-sul ad cus-tó-di-am.   A-men.
That with thy wont-ed fa-vour thou Wouldst be our guard and keep-er now.   A-men.

2 Procul recédant sómnia,
   Et nóctium phantásmata:
   Hostémque nostrum cómprime,
   Ne polluántur córpora.

3 Praesta Pater omnipotens,
   Per Jesum Christum Dóminum
   Qui tecum in perpétuum
   Regnat cum Sancto Spíritu. Amen.

2 From all ill dreams defend our eyes,
   From nightly fears and fantasies;
   Tread under foot our ghostly foe,
   That no pollution we may know.

3 O Father, that we ask be done,
   Through Jesus Christ, thine only Son;
   Who, with the Holy Ghost and thee
   Doth live and reign eternally. Amen.

This hymn is sung at the Office of Compline, a service which originated as a private bed-time devotion, introduced from the Eastern Church and recommended by St Benedict to his monks. In the Middle Ages Compline became a popular service, that is to say, people would come to the local church and listen to the service being sung by the clergy or by the monastic choir. It has remained to this day the best known and most popular of the Hours.

Nuns in choir

13   A Gregorian grace before meals

DOH = B♭
First note B♭

The ancient custom of the blessing of food and drink before meals links Christian practice with that of its parent religion, Judaism. Here is an old prayer taken from the more developed monastic *Benedicite*. The word 'benedicite', meaning 'bless', is taken from the opening word of this prayer and has passed into modern English as the name for grace at table. The word 'grace' itself also comes from a prayer — the prayer recited at the end of a meal to give thanks for the food and drink: 'Gratias agimus tibi' (we give thee thanks).

The flow and rhythm of the words with their accentuation, punctuation and phrasing, is the best guide to good interpretation.

Nuns in the refectory

14   Two prayers of thanksgiving

DOH = B♭
First note B♭

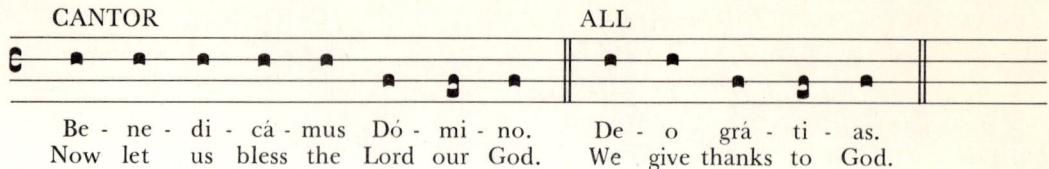

Be - ne - di - cá - mus Dó - mi - no.   De - o   grá - ti - as.
Now let   us   bless the Lord our God.   We give thanks to God.

DOH = C
First note G

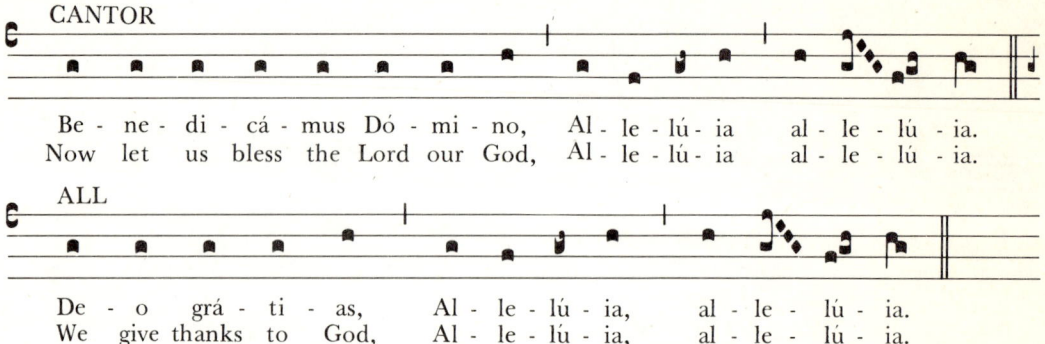

Be - ne - di - cá - mus Dó - mi - no,   Al - le - lú - ia   al - le - lú - ia.
Now let   us   bless the Lord our God, Al - le - lú - ia   al - le - lú - ia.

De - o   grá - ti - as,   Al - le - lú - ia,   al - le - lú - ia.
We give thanks to God,   Al - le - lú - ia,   al - le - lú - ia.

The first of these two prayers comes from grace or thanksgiving after meals. It is also sung at the end of each of the Little Hours (see the note to No. 11).

The second prayer is traditionally sung at the end of Lauds and Vespers at Easter time: this explains why it is followed by a joyful double *alleluia*.

Troping

The 'Benedicamus Domino, Deo gratias' versicle and response was often *troped*, that is, extra words were inserted. Some medieval Christmas pieces may be traced back to the practice of troping, see for instance the last two verses of the delightful 'Puer natus in Bethlehem' (No. 15).

15 A Christmas hymn *Puer natus*

DOH = D
First note E

Pu-er na-tus in Béth-le-hem, al-le-lú-ia: Un-de gáu-det
A boy is born in Beth-le-hem, al-le-lu-ia: There-fore re-joice,

Je-rú-sa-lem, al-le-lú-ia, al-le-lú-ia. ℟ In cor-dis jú-bi-lo
Je-ru-sa-lem, al-le-lu-ia, al-le-lu-ia. ℟ Our hearts are filled with joy,

Chri-stum na-tum a-do-ré-mus, Cum no-vo cán-ti-co.
To Christ the king, new ca-rols sing, To praise the new-born boy.

2 In carne nobis símilis, allelúia,
   Peccáto sed dissímilis, allelúia, allelúia
   (etc.)

3 In hoc natáli gáudio, allelúia,
   BENEDICÁMUS DÓMINO, allelúia,
   allelúia, (etc.)

4 Laudétur sancta Trínitas, allelúia,
   DEO dicámus GRÁTIAS, allelúia,
   allelúia, (etc.)

2 In flesh like ours he came to earth,
   alleluia,
   In sin alone unlike our birth, alleluia,
   alleluia, (etc.)

3 In this Nativity rejoice, alleluia,
   Now bless the Lord with single voice,
   alleluia, alleluia (etc.)

4 O praise the Holy Trinity, alleluia:
   Our thanks, Lord God, we sing to thee,
   alleluia, alleluia, (etc.)

Virgin and Child

16 Two antiphons for the dead – for the funeral of Phyllyp Sparowe

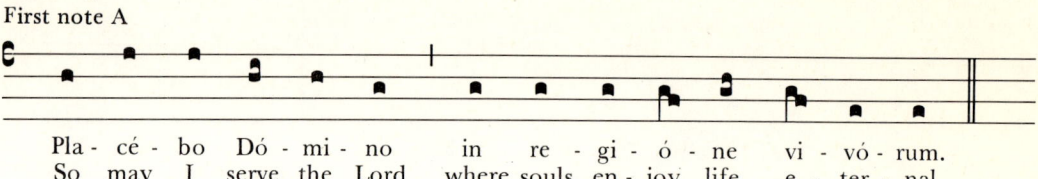

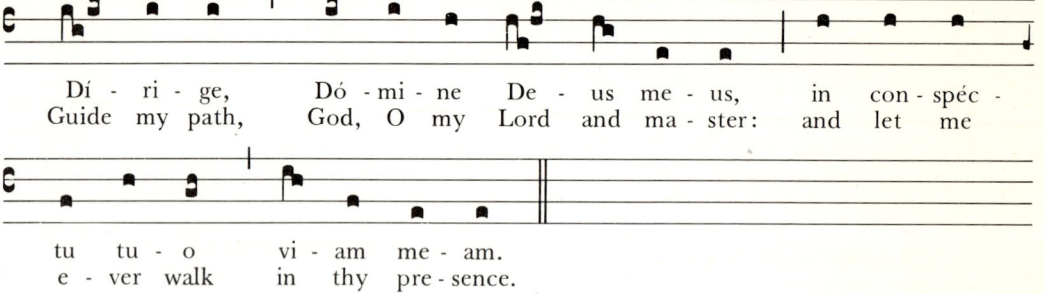

Pla ce bo,
    Who is there, who?
Di le xi,
    Dame Margery,
Fa, re, my, my.
    Wherefore and why why?
For the sowle of Philip Sparowe,
That was late slayn at Carowe,
Among the Nones Blake.

Girls used to be sent as boarders to Benedictine nunneries, and one of them, Jane Scrope, has achieved fame as the heroine of John Skelton's poem *Phyllyp Sparowe* (c. 1505–7, written when Skelton was Rector of Diss in Norfolk). Jane went to school at the Benedictine house of Carrow, on the outskirts of Norwich, and her pet sparrow, Philip, was slain by Gib, the convent cat. The poem is a mock elegy for Philip Sparrow, and it is punctuated by quotations from the well-known *Office of the Dead*, in their correct order of occurrence. It is all done so skilfully that if one knows the music one can imagine the service going on in the background as the girl laments her dead bird and invites all the birds of the forest to come and sing at the funeral.

Placebo, the opening word of the poem, is the opening antiphon of Vespers of the Dead. *Dirige*, which Skelton quotes in his 'addition' at the end of the poem, is the opening antiphon

of Matins, from which the modern word 'dirge' was derived. Towards the end of the Middle Ages it became increasingly fashionable to make provision in one's will for a priest to sing a *Requiem Mass* and the *Office of the Dead* for the repose of one's soul. Here is a typical extract from a will, that of Henry Philip, an Alderman of Oxford, dated 1459:

'Item, I bequeth to the parson of the said Churche of Saint Petres, being present at the Dirige & Masse, vi d. Item, to viij other prestes, being well disposed, there present to syng and Rede at the Dirige and Masse in the day of my Sepulture, to euery of the viij prestis, iiij d.'

17 A funeral chant *In paradisum*

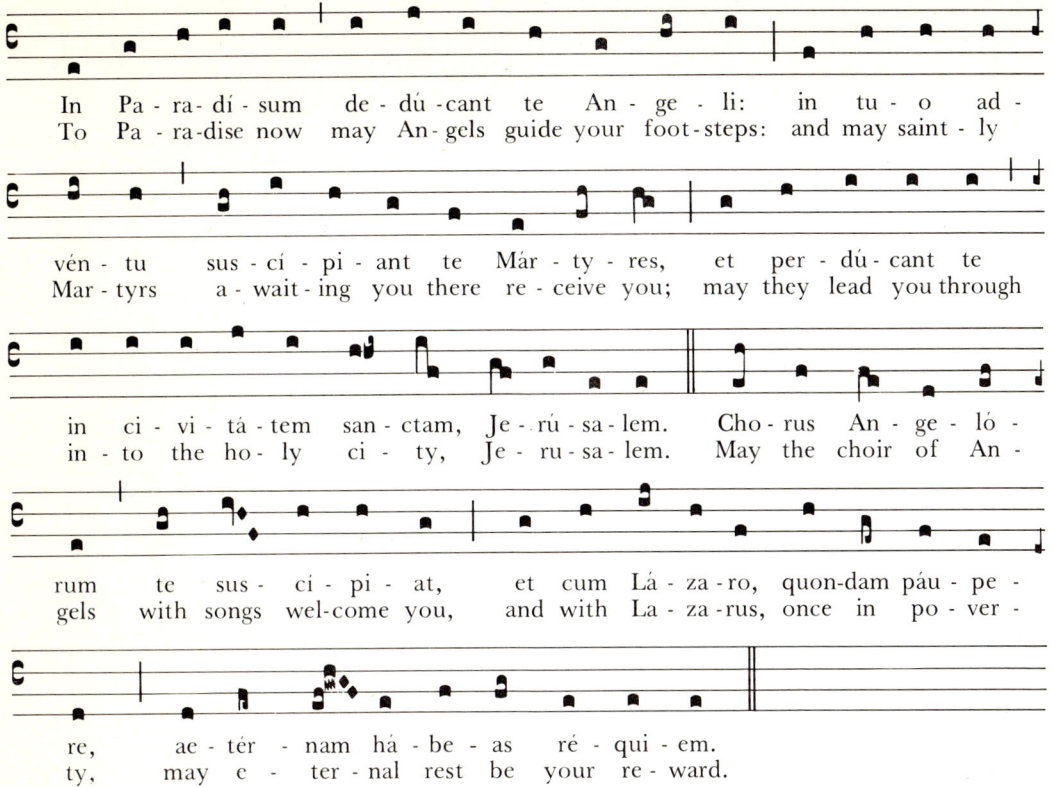

This is the chant that accompanies a man as he embarks upon his last journey — from the church to his final place of burial and repose. In contrast to the better known and awe-inspiring *Dies irae*, telling of the Last Judgment, this is a chant of serene peace and beauty. It is not surprising that it has captured the imagination of at least one twentieth century musician: the French composer Maurice Duruflé, who used it to great effect towards the end of his *Requiem Mass*.

The *liquescents* (see page 22) at 'sanctam', 'quondam' and 'æternam' need special care: the 'n', the 'm' and the 'r' should be sounded softly on these notes and only half-vocalized. The first syllable of 'sanctam' also has a light repercussion (see page 6)  approximately

which should be **sung rather smoothly**, not bounced.

Notice the final syllable of 'æternam' which has a group of no less than six notes, including a *quilisma*. This is not difficult if you work out the direction of the notes (low—high—higher—higher-still—low—lower) and remember that the two notes before the *quilisma* are slightly lengthened and the *quilisma* itself sung rather lightly, as a 'leading-note'. It could be transcribed approximately as follows using modern staff notation:

Give the group plenty of time to develop over the curve of the melody. Remember, too, that the 'h' that follows (at the beginning of 'habeas') is silent: you always have to drop your aitches in the Latin of the chant!

The song school

'I solfa and sing after, and is me nevere the nerre'
The Choristers' Lament
(MS Arundel 292, f. 70v, tr. Lee Utley)

18 A scripture reading

DOH = A
First note A
Deuteronomy 6: 4—7

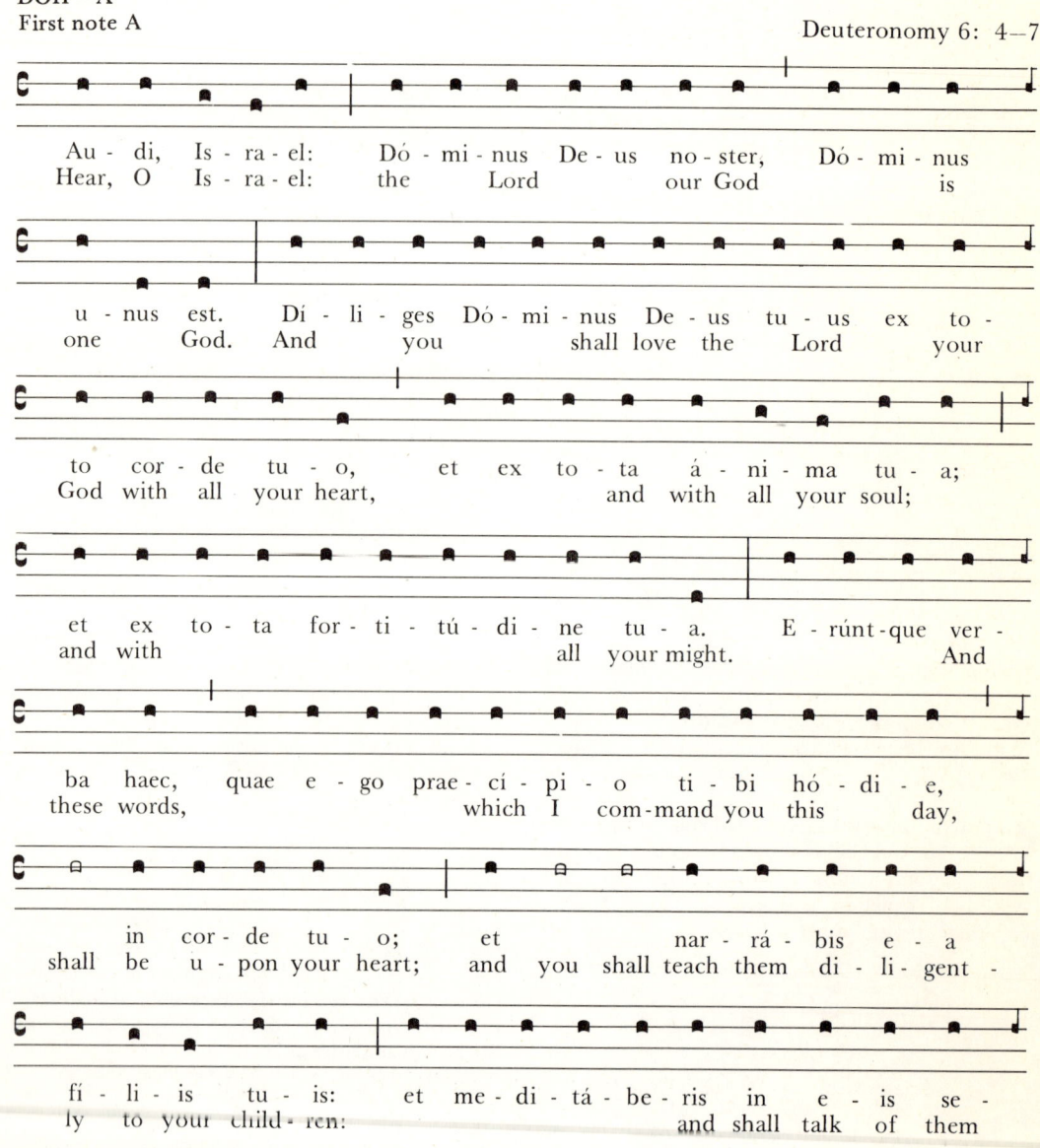

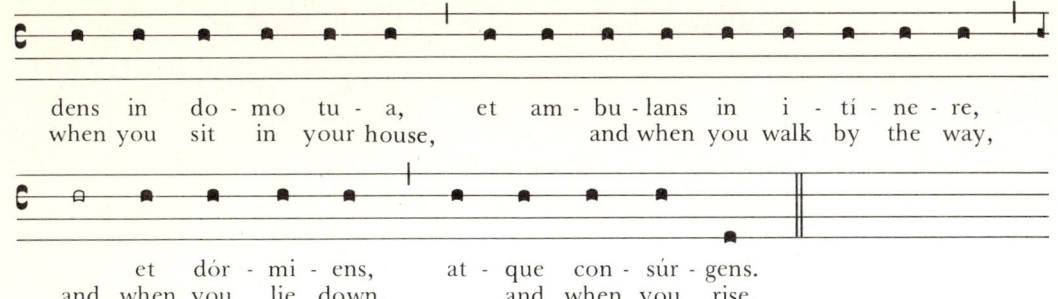

dens in do - mo tu - a, et am - bu - lans in i - ti - ne - re,
when you sit in your house, and when you walk by the way,

et dór - mi - ens, at - que con - súr - gens.
and when you lie down, and when you rise.

The song schools were the junior schools of earlier centuries. They may even be traced back to the first centuries of the Church when children learned to read and write by training to be lectors, or readers. And to read meant, of course, to chant aloud the books of the Bible. By the fourth century we read of groups of lectors sharing their training. Pope Liberius (352–66) started his ecclesiastical career as a child among a group of children all training to be lectors. Some of these children might even be as young as five years old.

The lector was soon to become a tonsured cleric in minor Orders and at his Ordination he received from the Bishop the book which symbolized his office. The lector read the lessons and proclaimed the prophecies to the assembly of the people, using the ancient technique of cantillation, inherited from the Jewish Synagogue.

We have here an example of one of the simple reading melodies. You will notice that the tune is nearly all on one note, a note which is called the 'reciting note', or 'tenor' (holder) — from which we have the modern word used to describe a high male voice. The melody drops down a fifth at every full-stop, in accordance with the natural tendency to drop one's voice at the end of a sentence. About half-way through a sentence there is a half-way, or mediant, cadence, and if the first half of the sentence is rather long an additional inflexion is made, dropping the voice a minor third, to enable the singer to make sense of his reading, and if necessary to take a breath.

Practise reading the texts, either in English or in Latin, in an ordinary speaking voice first, and then try them with the melody. You might wonder why people bothered to *sing* these texts and not just simply *speak* them. There are several reasons for this. In the first place, the singing voice carries far better than the speaking voice. It is also much less tiring to sing than to speak for long in a very loud voice. The third reason is that it is more solemn to sing than merely to speak, so a cantillation melody is something that adds beauty and solemnity to the reading.

When you have practised these texts (in Latin and in English) try adapting the tune to other words. Remember always to drop down a fifth for a full-stop.

Chanting the scriptures at Mass in an Abbey today. The music, gestures, and liturgical vestments are still very similar to those of medieval times.

19 A medieval teaching aid *Ut queant laxis*

Notice the FAH clef.
FAH = B♭
First note F

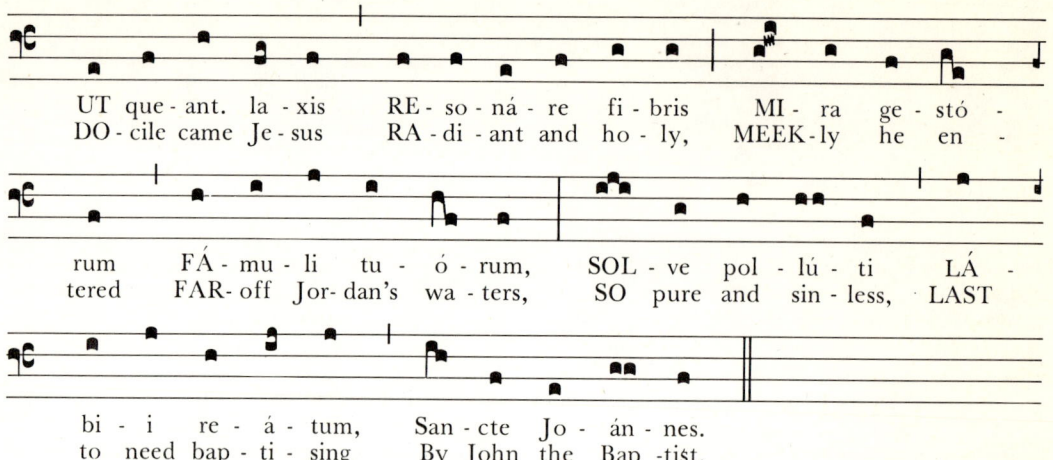

UT que - ant. la - xis   RE - so - ná - re   fi - bris   MI - ra   ge - stó -
DO - cile came Je - sus   RA - di - ant and ho - ly,   MEEK - ly he en -

rum   FÁ - mu - li tu - ó - rum,   SOL - ve pol - lú - ti   LÁ -
tered   FAR - off Jor - dan's wa - ters,   SO pure and sin - less,   LAST

bi - i re - á - tum,   San - cte Jo - án - nes.
to need bap - ti - sing   By John the Bap - tist.

Guido d'Arezzo was a famous teacher of music who lived in the eleventh century. He worked at the Benedictine monastery of Pomposa, Italy. One of his teaching aids for beginners was the hymn in honour of St John the Baptist, *Ut queant laxis*. Guido had noticed that each of the first six phrases of this tune begins on a new note of the rising major scale, so you hear in sequence — and remember — the sounds DOH–RAY–ME–FAH–SOH–LAH. The 'DOH' used to be called 'UT', and this is the clue to the Latin syllables used for the note names; they came originally from the beginning of each line of the first verse of this hymn:

Latin words
   UT queant laxis
   REsonáre fibris
   MIra gestórum
   FÁ muli tuorum,
   SOLve pullúti
   LÁbii reátum,
            Sancte Ioánnes.

English translation (not for singing)
   So that we may freely sing
   thy marvellous deeds,
   cleanse thy servants' lips
   from all stains of guilt,
            O blessed John.

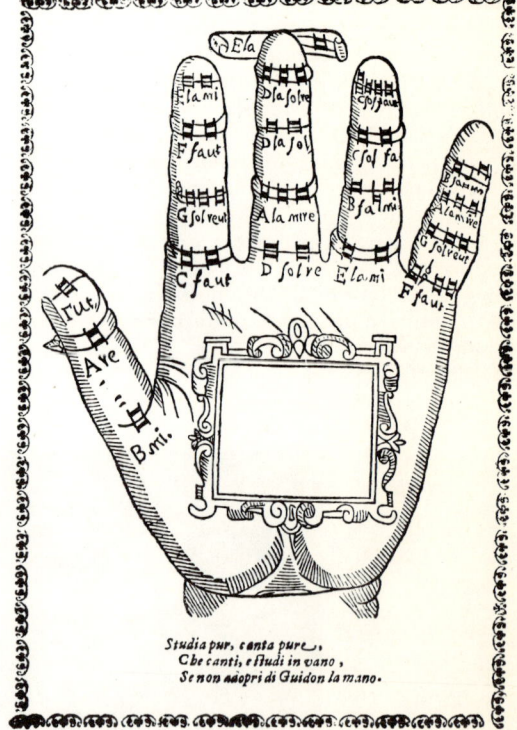

Guido's hand

In Guido's day, and for many centuries after him, musicians used a basic scale of six notes only, which could be transposed to begin on C, or G, or F (followed by B♭). The name of the seventh note of our modern major scale is said to be derived from the initials 'S' and 'I' of 'Sancte Ioannes', and of course the name 'SI' is still in common use in many European countries and in Latin America. In recent times it has been altered to 'TI' (or 'TE') in English-speaking countries in order to give greater incisiveness to the leading-note. Sight-singing to solfa names may not be familiar to many people, but it is well worth taking the trouble to practise it, as it is a great help in getting the semitones in the right places, between ME and FAH, and between TE and DOH.

Guido d'Arezzo taught his choristers the names of the notes of the scale by going round and round the left hand, pointing to finger-tips and joints, one for each note, from the G on the bottom line in the bass clef to the E in the fourth space in the treble clef. A boy would start with Gamma Ut on the tip of his left thumb and work down the thumb, then across the base of all the fingers, then up the little finger and across all the finger-tips, then down the forefinger and across the middle joints to the third finger, then back across the first joints of the third finger and the middle finger, and he finally flew off into space for the last note, E la (top E). The B in the second and third octaves could be either B♭ or B♮ and was called B fa – B mi, written ♭fa – ♮mi. This is the origin of our flat and natural signs.

Guido's Hand was used in teaching the notes of the scale for many centuries after the great master's death. The picture comes from a seventeenth-century Italian textbook and the motto is a warning that if you do not practise your solfa you may well find that you study and sing in vain.

Psalms

A boy in the song school had to learn the whole of his psalter off by heart, from Psalm 1 to Psalm 150. He learnt it gradually verse by verse, repeating each one after his master. Boys used to 'hear' each other as they went on journeys. They learnt as well the beautiful and varied psalm-tones to which the psalms were sung daily in choir during the Hour Services. There are tones for each of the eight modes (see page 8).

No. 20 is an example of a setting of Psalm 117, the shortest psalm of all. It is set to Tone V, which corresponds to the FAH mode, Mode V. Every psalm-tone is made up of two broad phrases. The first of these opens with the *intonation*, which is normally sung for the first verse only (except in the case of the New Testament canticles, such as the *Magnificat* and the *Nunc Dimittis*). The music rises to the reciting note for the words of the first half-verse, ending on a half-way, or mediant, cadence. The second phrase balances the first, starting on the reciting note for the text of the second half-verse and ending with a final cadence, which is also called a 'difference'. Notice that although this is Tone V it does not end on FAH, because the psalm would normally be sung with an *antiphon* (see No. 2) and the antiphon which was repeated at the end, would bring the whole piece — antiphon–psalm–antiphon — to a close on the tonic FAH.

How to sing a psalm

Start by reading the text, as naturally as possible, bringing out the accent lightly in each word, and thinking about the meaning of the words. Then practise the tune, until you know it by heart, with its two cadences falling gently to a close at the end of each half-verse. Then put words and music together. A solo cantor could intone the first verse as far as the asterisk and half the choir could continue this verse after a moment's pause. It is always important to make a good pause at the mediant cadence, long enough for the sound to die away completely. At the final cadence, no pause is needed other than just the time to take a quick breath. The other half of the choir sings verse 2. Then the first half of the choir sings verse 3, and so on, alternately, until the end of the psalm. Both halves of the choir can join forces to sing an antiphon, if there is one, before and after the psalm.

20 A psalm *Laudate Dominum*

DOH = B
First note E

1. Lau - dá - te Dó - mi - num om - nes gén - tes: lau - dá - te e - um
1. O praise the Lord   all ye hea - then: praise him

óm - nes pó - pu - li.   2. Quó - ni - am con - fir - má - ta est su - per
all ye na - tions.   2. For   his mer - ci - ful   kind - ness is

nos mi - se - ri - cór - di - a é - jus: et   vé - ri - tas Dó -
e - ver more and more   to - wards us: and the truth of the Lord

mi - ni ma - net in   ae - tér - num. 3. Gló - ri - a   Pa -
en - dur - eth for e - ver. 3. Glo - ry be to the Fa -

tri et Fí - li - o,   Et   Spi - ri - tu - i Sánc - to.
ther, and to the Son: And to the Ho - ly Spi - rit.

4. Sic - ut e - rat in prin - cí - pi - o, et nunc, et   sem - per,
4. As it was in the be - gin - ning,   is now and e - ver shall be,

Et in sáe - cu - la sae - cu - ló - rum. A - men.
     world with - out end.   A - men.

21 *Alma Redemptoris Mater*

Madame Eglantyne, Chaucer's Prioress on her way to Canterbury, tells the story of a small boy in the song school who hears the older boys singing the beautiful antiphon *Alma Redemptoris Mater*. The youngest choristers are not yet experienced enough to be taught this piece, but the boy so loves the sound of it that he persuades a senior chorister to teach him the antiphon after school. In the story the little chorister is kidnapped and murdered, but even after his death he continues to sing the *Alma Redemptoris Mater* and this leads to the discovery of the crime and the capture of the murderers.

Choristers used to be held in such high repute that if one of them died during his period of service he was buried with all the ceremonies due to a martyr. It may be from such practice that the numerous legends of martyred choirboys arose.

The version of the *Alma Redemptoris Mater* given here is taken from the *Barnwell Antiphoner*, a choir book used by the clergy of Barnwell Abbey, near Cambridge. It represents the Sarum Rite, or Rite of Salisbury Cathedral and would have been known and sung by boys in song schools all over England in Chaucer's day. At that time any man who could read and write would have started his education at the song school, unless he had been taught by a private tutor. Song schools were to be found attached to every cathedral and to many parish churches.

The melody as it appears in this Sarum source has one cadence which is of great beauty and which is not found in the normal Roman or monastic sources: the cadence at 'tuum sanctum Genitorem'. The introduction of the flattened seventh degree (TAW) is particularly striking: it changes the modality from the major mode to the SOH mode (transposed).

The *Alma Redemptoris Mater* dates from the eleventh century and has often been attributed to Herimannus Contractus, the lame monk of Reichenau.

Instruments

22 A motto for an organ loft

DOH = B♭
First note F

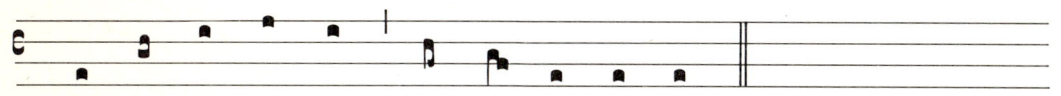

Om - nis spí - ri - tus   lau - det Dó - mi - num.
Let all that has breath praise, o praise the Lord.

'Omnis spiritus laudet Dominum'. This verse, from Psalm 150, is the last verse in the psalter, and it is sometimes to be found, most fittingly, inscribed over the console of a church organ. The pipe-organ has fulfilled an important role in the church for many centuries; it has, indeed, at times been the only instrument that one was allowed to introduce into the services. From the later Middle Ages onwards and well into the seventeenth and eighteenth centuries the organ had a recognized liturgical function: its 'voice' could be heard in alternation with the choir, often in brilliantly improvised passages based on the chant itself.

The short antiphon given here is sung at the Lauds of the Office of the Dead, together with the whole of Psalm 150. This psalm gives a brief catalogue of musical instruments with which the Psalmist invites the singers to praise the Lord.

23 An instrumental plainsong *In Nomine*

DOH = C
First note D

Gló - ri - a   ti - bi   Trí - ni - tas,   E - quá - lis   u - na   Dé - i - tas,
Glo - ry   to   you, O   Tri - ni - ty,   O   e - qual   and   sole   De - i - ty,

Et   an - te   óm - ni - a   sáe - cu - la,   Et   nunc et   in   per - pé - tu - um.
For,   Al - pha you are   be - fore all worlds, And   O - me - ga, Lord   of   a - ges.

♪ = 116

In the sixteenth century plainsong themes were often used as a basis (or *canto fermo*) for instrumental composition. Other parts were woven around the theme to form a beautiful and intricate polyphonic structure. A popular tune to be so used was the first antiphon from Vespers of Trinity Sunday, *Gloria tibi Trinitas*. Pieces built upon this theme bore the title *In Nomine*, from the *Benedictus* in Taverner's Mass on the same melody, where the section 'In nomine Domini' states the theme with perfect clarity, in notes of equal length. Byrd, Tallis and Tye were among the many English composers to write an instrumental *In Nomine*, and these compositions are still the delight of viol players and other lovers of early music.

This antiphon could be played on the violin or the recorder, or it could be sung to its original words. There are also numerous examples of keyboard settings, notably those in the *Mulliner Book* and in the *Fitzwilliam Virginal Book*.

In the setting given here by John Taverner (c. 1495–1545), arranged for four recorders by Francis Cameron, the chant will be found in the treble part, in notes of equal value (minims).

In Nomine arranged for four recorders

*Play F natural if F sharp is impossible.

© 1959 by Schott & Co. Ltd., London

The enthroning

Pageantry

24 The Laudes regiae, or Royal Acclamations *Christus vincit*

DOH = C
First note A

First time CANTORS repeated by ALL

Chri-stus vin - cit, Chri-stus re-gnat, Chri-stus ím-pe-rat. Ex-áu-di Chri-ste. Sum-mo pon-tí-fi-ci et u-ni-ver-sá-li Pa-pae vi-ta. Sal-vá-tor mun-di, Tu il-lum ád-ju-va. San-cte Pe-tre, Tu il-lum ád-ju-va. San-cte Cle-mens, Tu il-lum ád-ju-va. San-cte Six-te, Tu il-lum ád-ju-va. Chri-stus vin-cit, Chri-stus re-gnat, Chri-stus ím-pe-rat. Ex-áu-di Chri-ste. Re-gi An-gló-rum, a De-o co-ro-ná-to, sa-lus et vic-tó-ri-a. Re-dém-ptor mun-di, Tu il-lum ád-ju-va. San-cte AEd-mún-de, Tu (etc.)

Christ is vic-tor, Christ is rul-er, Christ is em-pe-ror. O hear our prayer Christ. To the high pon-tiff and un-i-ver-sal Ho-ly Fa-ther long life. Sa-viour of all men, Grant help and strength to him. Saint Pe-ter, Grant help and strength to him. Saint Cle-ment, Grant help and strength to him. Saint Six-tus, Grant help and strength to him. Christ is vic-tor, Christ is ru-ler, Christ is em-pe-ror. O hear our prayer, Christ. To the King of Eng-land, an-noin ted and crowned by God, grant long life and vic-to-ry. Re deem-er of men, Grant help and strength to him. Saint... Ed-mund, Grant (etc.)

41

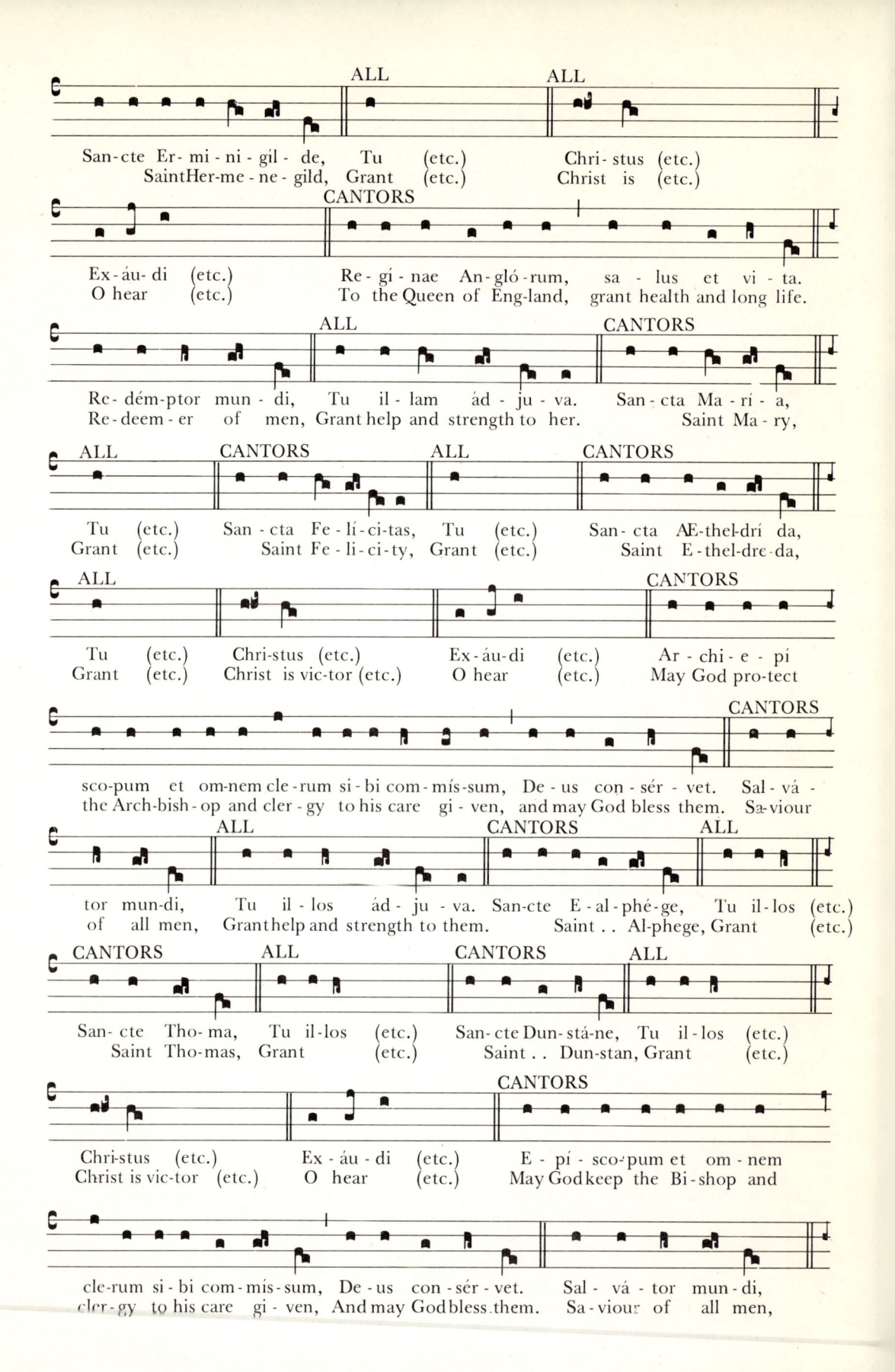

	ALL	ALL
San-cte Er-mi-ni-gíl-de,	Tu (etc.)	Chri-stus (etc.)
SaintHer-me-ne-gild,	Grant (etc.)	Christ is (etc.)

CANTORS

Ex-áu-di (etc.) Re-gí-nae An-gló-rum, sa-lus et vi-ta.
O hear (etc.) To the Queen of Eng-land, grant health and long life.

ALL CANTORS

Re-dém-ptor mun-di, Tu il-lam ád-ju-va. San-cta Ma-rí-a,
Re-deem-er of men, Grant help and strength to her. Saint Ma-ry,

ALL CANTORS ALL CANTORS

Tu (etc.) San-cta Fe-lí-ci-tas, Tu (etc.) San-cta Æ-thel-drí-da,
Grant (etc.) Saint Fe-li-ci-ty, Grant (etc.) Saint E-thel-dre-da,

ALL CANTORS

Tu (etc.) Chri-stus (etc.) Ex-áu-di (etc.) Ar-chi-e-pí
Grant (etc.) Christ is vic-tor (etc.) O hear (etc.) May God pro-tect

CANTORS

sco-pum et om-nem cle-rum si-bi com-mís-sum, De-us con-sér-vet. Sal-vá-
the Arch-bish-op and cler-gy to his care gi-ven, and may God bless them. Sa-viour

ALL CANTORS ALL

tor mun-di, Tu il-los ád-ju-va. San-cte E-al-phé-ge, Tu il-los (etc.)
of all men, Grant help and strength to them. Saint .. Al-phege, Grant (etc.)

CANTORS ALL CANTORS ALL

San-cte Tho-ma, Tu il-los (etc.) San-cte Dun-stá-ne, Tu il-los (etc.)
Saint Tho-mas, Grant (etc.) Saint .. Dun-stan, Grant (etc.)

CANTORS

Chri-stus (etc.) Ex-áu-di (etc.) E-pí-sco-pum et om-nem
Christ is vic-tor (etc.) O hear (etc.) May God keep the Bi-shop and

cle-rum si-bi com-mís-sum, De-us con-sér-vet. Sal-vá-tor mun-di,
cler-gy to his care gi-ven, And may God bless them. Sa-viour of all men,

ALL   **CANTORS**   **ALL**   **CANTORS**

Tu il-los (etc.)   San-cte Os-wál-de,   Tu il-los (etc.)   San-cte Wul-stá-ne,
Grant   (etc.)   Saint.. Os-wald,   Grant   (etc.)   Saint.. Wul-stan,

ALL   * **CANTORS**   **ALL**   **CANTORS**

Tu il-los (etc.)   San-cte Eg-wi-ne,   Tu il-los (etc.)   Chri-stus (etc.)
Grant   (etc.)   Saint.. Eg-win,   Grant   (etc.)   Christ is vic-tor (etc.)

CANTORS

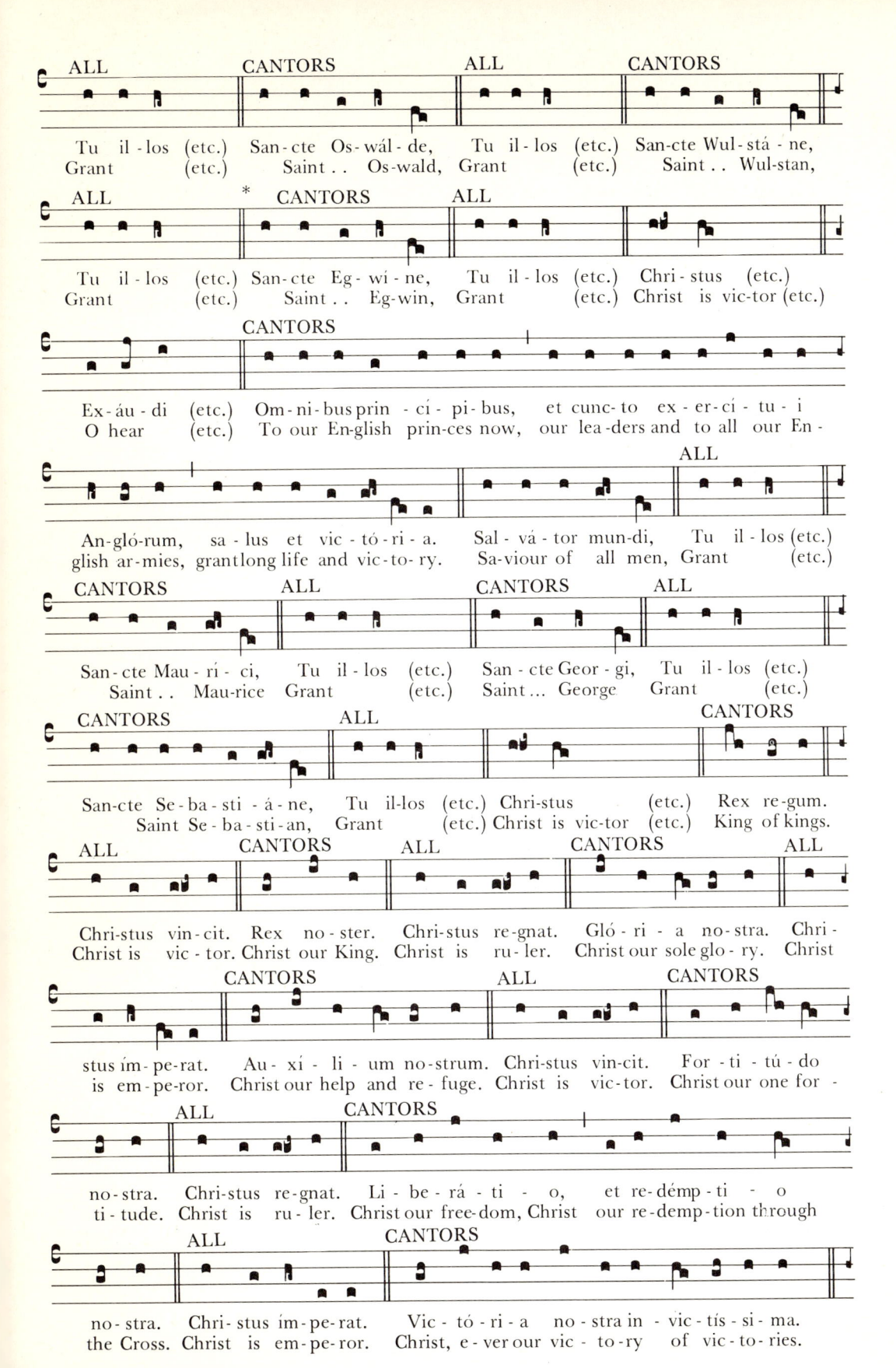

Ex-áu-di (etc.)   Om-ni-bus prin-ci-pi-bus,   et cunc-to ex-er-ci-tu-i
O hear (etc.)   To our En-glish prin-ces now,   our lea-ders and to all our En-

                                                     ALL

An-gló-rum,   sa-lus et vic-tó-ri-a.   Sal-vá-tor mun-di,   Tu il-los (etc.)
glish ar-mies, grant long life and vic-to-ry.   Sa-viour of all men,   Grant   (etc.)

CANTORS   **ALL**   **CANTORS**   **ALL**

San-cte Mau-ri-ci,   Tu il-los (etc.)   San-cte Geor-gi,   Tu il-los (etc.)
Saint.. Mau-rice   Grant   (etc.)   Saint... George   Grant   (etc.)

CANTORS   **ALL**   **CANTORS**

San-cte Se-ba-sti-á-ne,   Tu il-los (etc.) Chri-stus (etc.)   Rex re-gum.
Saint Se-ba-sti-an,   Grant (etc.) Christ is vic-tor (etc.)   King of kings.

ALL   **CANTORS**   **ALL**   **CANTORS**   **ALL**

Chri-stus vin-cit. Rex no-ster. Chri-stus re-gnat. Gló-ri-a no-stra. Chri-
Christ is vic-tor. Christ our King. Christ is ru-ler. Christ our sole glo-ry. Christ

             CANTORS   **ALL**   **CANTORS**

stus im-pe-rat. Au-xi-li-um no-strum. Chri-stus vin-cit. For-ti-tú-do
is em-pe-ror. Christ our help and re-fuge. Christ is vic-tor. Christ our one for-

ALL   **CANTORS**

no-stra. Chri-stus re-gnat. Li-be-rá-ti-o, et re-démp-ti-o
ti-tude. Christ is ru-ler. Christ our free-dom, Christ our re-demp-tion through

ALL   **CANTORS**

no-stra. Chri-stus im-pe-rat. Vic-tó-ri-a no-stra in-vic-tís-si-ma.
the Cross. Christ is em-pe-ror. Christ, e-ver our vic-to-ry of vic-to-ries.

*In the manuscript St. Dunstan is invoked at this point for the second time; he was, in fact, Bishop of Worcester before becoming Archbishop of Canterbury.

ALL: Chri-stus vin-cit. **CANTORS:** Mu-rus no-ster in-ex-pu-gná-bi-lis. **ALL:** Chri-stus re-gnat.
Christ is vic-tor. Christ our for-tress and Christ our safe strong-hold. Christ is ru-ler.

CANTORS: De-fén-si-o et ex-ul-tá-ti-o no-stra. **ALL:** Chri-stus im-pe-rat. **CANTORS:** Ip-si
Christ, sure de-fence and for e-ter-ni-ty our joy. Christ is em-pe-ror. Christ, do-

so-li im-pé-ri-um, gló-ri-a et po-té-stas, per im-mor-tá-li-a
mi-nion and rule be yours, glo-ry might and power be yours, through all e-ter-ni-ty,

sé-cu-la se-cu-ló-rum. A-men. **ALL:** Chri-stus vin-cit, Chri-stus re-gnat,
un-to a-ges and a-ges. A-men. Christ is vic-tor, Christ is ru-ler,

Chri-stus im-pe-rat. **CANTORS:** Ip-si so-li laus et ju-bi-lá-ti-o, et be-ne-
Christ is em-pe-ror. Christ, to you a-lone be ju-bi-la-tion, and praise and bles-

díc-ti-o, per in-fi-ní-ta sé-cu-la se-cu-ló-rum, A-men. **ALL:** Chri-stus vin-cit,
sing be yours, for e-ver-more and un-to a-ges and a-ges. A-men. Christ is vic-tor,

Chri-stus re-gnat, Chri-stus im-pe-rat. **CANTORS:** Ip-si so-li ho-nor et clá-ri-tas,
Christ is ru-ler, Christ is em-pe-ror. Christ, to you a-lone be ho-nour, and fame

et sa-pi-én-ti-a, per in-fi-ní-ta sé-cu-la se-cu-ló-rum. A-men.
and wis-dom yours a-lone, for e-ver-more and un-to a-ges and a-ges. A-men.

ALL: Chri-stus vin-cit, Chri-stus re-gnat, Chri-stus im-pe-rat.
Christ is vic-tor, Christ is ru-ler, Chirst is em-pe-ror.

These triumphant acclamations have been sung ever since the time of Charlemagne (742–814), himself a conqueror, a king and an emperor. Versions of them can be traced to many corners of the Frankish Empire. They were sung on great and joyful public occasions, such as coronations, and also to add solemnity to the major feast days of the Church, Christmas, Easter and

Whitsunday. The *Laudes* often followed the singing of the *Gloria* in the Mass. One by one, Pope, King, Queen and Bishop were acclaimed and placed under the protection of specially chosen saints. Here is an example of the *Laudes* as sung in medieval England: they come from Worcester Cathedral (MS F 160). The saints invoked for the Pope are his earliest predecessors, Peter, Clement and Sixtus. For the King of England, three royal saints are chosen: Edmund, Hermenegild and the Northumbrian martyr, Oswald. The Queen is placed under the special protection of the Virgin Mary, the Roman matron Felicity, and the East Anglian princess, Etheldreda. The Archbishop and his clergy are protected by three former Archbishops of Canterbury, Alphege, Thomas à Becket and Dunstan. The Bishop of Worcester, very properly, has saints from his own diocese, Oswald the Bishop, Wulfstan, Dunstan again, and Egwin. The princes and armies of the realm are given protectors with military associations: Maurice, the leader of the Theban Legion, and the two martyrs George, the Patron Saint of England, and Sebastian, who was shot to death by archers.

The singing of the *Laudes* was generally led by two of the finest singers with strong, firm voices. These priests would be answered by the entire congregation. The festive character of the chant demanded loud and hearty singing; and this is borne out in the instructions contained in the sources.

On the first syllable of *Christus*, and indeed, throughout the acclamations, this little figure occurs: ♪ and you will remember that it indicates both a repercussion and a *liquescent* (here to help you to get your tongue round the letters 'ist'). There are many other examples of *liquescents*, all of which will be familiar to you by now. Curiously enough, this thirteenth-century manuscript from Worcester is inconsistent in its manner of notating some of the acclamations. For instance,

Tu il - lum ád - ju - va

becomes

Tu il - lam ád - ju - va

in the feminine (for the Queen), and when written in the masculine plural (for the Archbishop and clergy, etc.) these variants are found:

Tu il - los

or

Tu il - los

or

Tu il - los

As for the *Christus vincit* refrain itself, this begins broadly with its full decoration

Chri - stus vin - cit (etc.)

but towards the end of the piece it is reduced to

Chri - stus vin - cit, Chri - stus re - gnat, Chri - stus im - pe - rat.

which suggests much greater speed and conciseness — caused, no doubt, by the mounting tension and excitement.

In the transcription some slight rationalization of these variants has had to be introduced to make the piece easier to sing. But it does not seem possible to explain them away altogether as a form of shorthand used by the scribe. On the contrary, the fact that the variants exist leads one to think that the scribe was writing from memory his vivid recollection of actual performance, and this suggests the way in which the style of singing can be reconstructed. Start off with great pomp and majesty, then let the crowd's acclamations gather momentum and enthusiasm, so that the excitement continues to grow right up to the final climax.

You might like to reconstruct the whole magnificent scene of medieval pageantry as you sing these splendid acclamations, and to mime the King and Queen seated on their thrones with crowns on their heads, surrounded by the Archbishop, the Bishop of Worcester, the clergy, the monks and the nobility, and the people crowding round into the nave of the cathedral. Then the cantors would advance towards the throne to sing their solo parts, and all the crowd would reply in one tremendous chorus of sound.

Suggestions for further activities

1. Listen to the record *Jubilate Deo* (French Decca, 7552), following the music in the booklet, *Jubilate Deo*, London, Catholic Truth Society, 1974.
2. If your choir enjoys music by contemporary composers, learn to sing Benjamin Britten's version of *Hodie* in his *Ceremony of Carols*, published by Boosey and Hawkes. Try to get a harp rather than a piano to accompany you, so that you can hear what the chant sounds like with an original modern accompaniment.
3. Try to find some other pieces by contemporary composers based on plainsong, for instance, Duruflé's *Requiem* which makes exquisite use of the *In paradisum*.
4. Play, or listen to some of the pieces with plainsong titles in a modern edition of the *Fitzwilliam Virginal Book*, or the *Mulliner Book*. See if you can make out the plainsong tunes and sing them.
5. If there is an abbey in your neighbourhood where they sing Gregorian chant, go and hear some live singing (for example, at Ampleforth, Downside, Farnborough, Prinknash, Ryde or Quarr in England, Pluscarden in Scotland, or Argentan, Solesmes, Saint-Wandrille, Bec Hellouin, Kergonan in France, or Hauterive in Switzerland).
6. Make an expedition to the nearest ruined abbey or medieval church and sing some chant there (for example, in the choir at Fountains).
7. Pieces to play on your recorder include: *Hortus Musicus* No. 134, published by Bärenreiter, which gives seven settings of *In Nomines* in four and five parts for recorders by Taverner, Whyte, Johnson, Baldwin, Bull, and two by Tye; two settings by Purcell for six and seven instruments which have been edited for recorders by Walter Bergmann and published by Faber Music; *Gregorian Chants for the Recorder*, by Stuart Isacoff (Wise Publications), settings of plainsong from medieval times onwards, from works by composers such as Machaut, Dufay, Josquin, Palestrina and Bach, which are edited and arranged for solo, duet and trio playing for soprano, alto or tenor recorder.

Background reading

Books

Abraham, Gerald (ed.). *New Oxford History of Music*, Vol. IV, *The Age of Humanism, 1540–1630* (London, Oxford University Press, 1968). Useful information about the composers of *In Nomines*.

Apel, Willi. *Gregorian Chant* (Bloomington and London, Indiana University Press, 1958. 5th printing, 1973). An original study, indispensable for anyone wishing to delve deep into the subject.

Caldwell, John. *Medieval Music* (London, Hutchinson, 1978).

Chaucer, Geoffrey. *The Prioress' Prologue and Tale from the Canterbury Tales*, edited with introduction, notes and glossary by J. Winny (Cambridge University Press, 1975). This is the story of the 'Little clergeon' who chants the *Alma Redemptoris Mater*.

Corbin, Solange. *L'Eglise à la Conquête de sa Musique* (Paris, Gallimard, 1960). For anyone with fluent French this is a scholarly study written in a lively style.

Harman, Alec, Wilfrid Mellers and Anthony Milner. *Man and his Music* (London, Barrie and Rockliff, 1962).

Harrison, Frank Lloyd. *Music in Medieval Britain* (London, Routledge and Kegan Paul, 1958). This gives a wealth of information about the liturgical and institutional background.

Hughes, Dom Anselm (ed.). *New Oxford History of Music*, Vol. II, *Early Medieval Music up to 1300* (London, Oxford University Press, 1954).

Hughes, Dom Anselm and Gerald Abraham (eds.). *New Oxford History of Music*, Vol. III, *Ars Nova and the Renaissance 1300–1540* (London, Oxford University Press, 1960).

Kantorowicz, Ernst Hartwig. *Laudes regiae* (Berkeley University Press, California, 1946; 2nd printing, 1958). A scholarly study of the history of the festive *Laudes*.

Knowles, David. *Bare Ruined Choirs* (Cambridge University Press, 1976). An account of English monasticism at the time of the Dissolution of the Monasteries.

Loomis, L.R., *The Council of Constance* (New York, Columbia University Department of Historical Records of Civilization: Sources and Studies, 1961). Contains translations of Richental's Chronicle, Fillastre's Diary and Cerrentone's Journal.

Marrocco, W. Thomas and Nicholas Sandon (eds.). *The Oxford Anthology of Music: Medieval Music.* (London, Oxford University Press, 1977). Contains some fifty pages of chant including the whole of the Procession before Mass, and the Mass itself, on Easter Day at Salisbury Cathedral.

Robertson, Alec and Denis Stevens. *Pelican History of Music*, Vol I (Harmondsworth, Penguin Books, 1960). Contains a good introductory chapter on the chant.

Skelton, John. *Poems*, ed. Robert S. Kinsman (London, Oxford University Press, 1969). This gives the complete poem about the funeral of Phyllyp Sparowe.

Thompson, Alexander Hamilton. *Song-Schools in the Middle Ages* (London, Church Music Society, 1942). Contains much useful information about the lives of choristers.

Werner, Eric. *The Sacred Bridge*, The Interdependence of Liturgy and Music in Synagogue and Church during the First Millenium. (London, Dennis Dobson; New York, Columbia University Press, 1959).

Wilkinson, John. *Egeria's Travels*. Newly translated with supporting documents and notes. (London, Society for the Promotion of Christian Knowledge, 1971). A fascinating account of early church services in Jerusalem.

Specialist articles

Bent, Ian. 'The English Chapel Royal before 1300' (*Proceedings of the Royal Musical Association*, Vol. XC, 1963/4, 75–95).

Bowles, Edmund A. 'The Organ in the Medieval Liturgical Service' (*Revue Belge de Musicologie*, Vol. XVI, 1962, 13–29).

Caldwell, John. 'Keyboard Plainsong Settings in England, 1500–1660' (*Musica Disciplina*, Vol. XIX, 1965, 129–53).

Corbin, Solange. 'La Cantillation des Rituels Chrétiens' (*Revue de Musicologie*, Vol. XLVII, 1961, 3–36).

Harrison, Frank Lloyd. 'Benedicamus, Conductus, Carol: A Newly Discovered Source' (*Acta Musicologica*, Vol. XXXVII, 1965, 35–48).

Lee-Utley, F. 'The Choristers' Lament' (MS Arundel 292, Late fourteenth century, *Speculum*, Vol. XVI, 1946, 194ff).

Records

A wide choice of recordings of Gregorian chant is available. With the exception of the record on the modes, all those suggested below contain chants from this book, not always, however, in exactly the same version. Sometimes, for example, the monastic choirs sing from their monastic version, whereas we give the Sarum or the Roman version. It will be interesting to sing our version first and then to listen to the record. See what differences there are, if any, and which version you prefer.

Choeur des Moines de Kergonan (Benedictine Monks, and Boys from Junior Choir of Foyer Notre Dame de Pontcalec). The recording includes *Ut queant laxis* and *In paradisum*. (SM 30 S-515)

Choix d'Hymnes (Benedictine Nuns of Notre Dame d'Argentan). Includes *Conditor*, *Vexilla regis* and *Ut queant laxis*. (French Decca 7557)

Gesänge zu Marienfesten (Schola Cantorum Francesco Coradini, Arezzo). Includes the *Alma Redemptoris Mater* (but not the Sarum version the 'little clergeon' knew). (Archiv 2533 310)

L'Histoire du Salut I L'Attente (Argentan). Includes *Hodie*. (French Decca 7506)

L'Histoire du Salut II La Rédemption (Argentan). Gives the Easter Responsory *Surrexit*. (French Decca 7507)

Jubilate Deo (Argentan). Includes the first *Alleluia* and the *Veni creator*. (French Decca 7552)

La Messe de la Sainte Trinité (Monks of Solesmes). Has the *Alleluia Benedictus* (No. 3). (French Decca 7547)

Les Modes Grégoriennes (Argentan). Contains examples of typical pieces in each of the eight modes. (French Decca 7518a)

Purification de la Sainte Vierge – Notre Dame des Sept Douleurs (Argentan). Candlemas music. (French Decca 7526)

Semaine de la Pentecôte (Argentan). Contains the hymn *Veni creator*. (French Decca 7520A)

Vendredi Saint (Monks of Solesmes). Includes the *Trisagion* (Hagios o Theos). (French Decca 7512A)

Sources

Chants

Abbreviations

AM	*Antiphonale Monasticum* (Desclée, Tournai 1934)
BCP	*Book of Common Prayer*
GR	*Graduale Romanum*, the new official Vatican edition of the Roman Gradual, following the 1974 revision (Desclée, Tournai, 1974).
JMN	translated by John Mason Neale
LU	*Liber Usualis*, a fairly comprehensive collection of chants from the Roman Antiphonale and the Roman Graduale (Desclée, Tournai, 1962).
MB	translated by Mary Berry
NEB	*New English Bible*
RHMcC	translated by Rose Mary McCabe
RSV	*Revised Standard Version*
SA	*Antiphonale Sarisburiense*, a facsimile edition of a thirteenth-century manuscript from Barnwell Abbey, near Cambridge, Cambridge University Library MS. MM.2.g (Plainsong and Mediaeval Music Society, London 1901–24; republished 1966 by Gregg Press, Farnborough).

1 Words seventh century, anon.; translation JMN; melody SA. 2 Words from Christmas Office of Vespers; translation RHMcC; melody LU. 3 Words Luke 2: 22–39; translation RHMcC & BCP; melody LU. 4 Words Venantius Fortunatus (530–609); translation JMN; melody Sarum rite from *English Hymnal*. 5 Words Luke 24: 34; translation MB; melody AM. 6(a) Words Luke 24: 29; translation MB; melody AM. 6(b) Words Psalm 118: 24; translation MB & BCP; melody AM. 7 Words before the tenth century; translation RHMcC & MB; melody GR. 8 Words from the Ordinary of the Mass; melody GR. 9 Words from the Liturgy of Good Friday; translation MB; melody GR. 10(a) From Lauds of Easter Vigil; melody AM. 10(b) From Lauds of Low Sunday; melody AM. 10(c) From the Proper of the Mass for Ember Saturday during Whitsuntide and for Trinity Sunday; melody GR; neums from St Gall MS 359. 11 Words from Office of Prime, fifth century; translation JMN; melody AM. 12 Words before the eighth century, Compline hymn; translation JMN; melody AM. 13 Words and melody from traditional monastic sources (Solesmes); translation RHMcC & MB. 14 Words from Monastic Office; translation RHMcC & MB; melody AM. 15 Benedicamus Trope; words and music *Cantus Selecti* (Tournai, Desclée et Cie, 1949); translation RHMcC. 16(a) Words from Vespers of the Dead, Psalm 116: 9; translation RHMcC; melody SA. 16(b) Words from Matins of the Dead, Psalm 5: 8; translation RHMcC; melody SA. 17 Words from Liturgy of the Dead; translation RHMcC; melody LU. 18 Words Deuteronomy 6: 4–7; translation RSV; melody from traditional sources: tone for the Lectio Brevis (Short Lesson). 19 Words and music by Paul the Deacon, a Monk of Monte Cassino (740–801); translation RHMcC & MB; melody AM. 20 Words Psalm 117; translation BCP; melody from traditional sources: Tone V. 21 Words and music eleventh century (attributed to Hermann the Lame, a Monk of Reichenau); translation RHMcC; melody SA. 22 Words from Lauds of the Dead, Psalm 150: 6; translation MB & RHMcC; melody LU. 23(a) Words from Vespers of the Trinity; translation RHMcC & MB; melody SA. 23(b) This setting, together with one by Blitheman, can be found in Schott's *Recorder Bibliothek* No. 10. 24 Words and music from a thirteenth-century manuscript in Worcestral Cathedral Library (MS F 160); translation RHMcC & MB; melody newly transcribed for this book.

Illustrations

Front cover, Luttrell Psalter, British Library; Title page, Psalter of Henry VI, British Library, MS Cotton Dom, A XVII, fol. 122v.; p. 7, Fourteenth-century gradual from Lessness Abbey, Kent, Victoria and Albert Museum, no. 23820; p. 8, Book of Hours, Bibliothèque Nationale, Paris, MS lat. 1176, fol. 132r.; p. 10, La Sainte Abbaye, British Library, MS Add. 39843, fol. 6v.; p. 14, *Processionale ad usum insignis ad praeclare ecclesiae sarum*; p. 19, Sarum Breviary, Bibliothèque Nationale, Paris, MS lat. 17294, fol. 497r.; p. 24, Poor Clares from Psalter of Henry VI, British Library, MS Cotton Dom. A XVII, fol. 74v.; p. 25, Poor Clares in *Polyptich of the Blessed Umilta* by Pietro Lorenzetti, Florence, fourteenth century (photo Alinari); p. 27, Terracotta by Antonio Rossellino, Victoria and Albert Museum; p. 28, *Antiphonale Sarisburiense* (see Abbreviations list above); p. 31, Quarr Abbey (photo Peter Matthews); p. 32, Scala di musica molto necessaria per principianti, *De Horatio Scaletta da Crema*, Bracciano, 1642; p. 33, British Library, 2.B.VII, fol. 291; p. 36, Carving by Luca della Robbia, Mansell Collection; p. 37, Painting by Memling, Mansell Collection; p. 40, Queen Mary's Psalter, British Library.